Spenser Wilkinson

British policy in South Africa

Spenser Wilkinson

British policy in South Africa

ISBN/EAN: 9783743384217

Manufactured in Europe, USA, Canada, Australia, Japa

Cover: Foto ©Suzi / pixelio.de

Manufactured and distributed by brebook publishing software (www.brebook.com)

Spenser Wilkinson

British policy in South Africa

BRITISH POLICY

IN

SOUTH AFRICA

BY

SPENSER WILKINSON

LONDON
SAMPSON LOW, MARSTON & COMPANY
LIMITED
St. Dunstan's House
FETTER LANE, FLEET STREET, E.C.
1899.

GIFT OF

PROFESSOR C. A. KOFOID

LONDON:
PRINTED BY WILLIAM CLOWES AND SONS, LIMITED,
STAMFORD STREET AND CHARING CROSS.

PREFACE.

THIS volume is an attempt to apply to a practical question of current politics the view of British policy which in previous essays the author has endeavoured to set forth and to justify. The South African crisis is perhaps not yet at an end; but the reader to whom the account here given of its nature commends itself will have little difficulty in forming his opinion with regard to the phases of the action which may still be to come.

When President Kruger and the Burghers of the Transvaal prove that they have abandoned their oligarchical system, and are willing to make a lasting settlement by accepting the Uitlanders as an integral part of their body politic, Great Britain may cease her preparations and attend to other questions; but it would be a mistake to think of peace until there is some guarantee of a complete change in the Boer policy.

The chapters appeared, between July 12 and July 19, as articles in the 'Morning Post,' and it is a pleasure to thank the proprietor of that newspaper for his kind permission to reprint them.

July 22, 1899.

CONTENTS.

CHAPTER I.

THE PROBLEM.

Democracy and Empire—Duty in the Management of an Empire—Why Great Britain must obtain fair Treatment for the Uitlanders—A Preliminary Survey of the Case—The Unity of South Africa—The Bases of Boer Rights—The Violation of the Spirit of the Compact—Great Britain's Obligations to her own People 1

CHAPTER II.

THE ORIGIN OF SOUTH AFRICA'S TROUBLES.

The General Conditions in South Africa—Close of the Reactionary Period—Liberalism and Emancipation—The Backward Policy Begins—First Effect: The Great Trek—Why did British Governments go Back? 17

CHAPTER III.

1877–1881: ORDERS, COUNTER-ORDERS, DISORDERS.

Lord Carnarvon's Policy—Backwards Once More—Why the Transvaal was Annexed—Mr. Gladstone in Opposition—Mr. Gladstone in Office—The Surrender—The Loyal Inhabitants—Mr. Gladstone's Pledge—The Fulfilment 34

CHAPTER IV.

PEACE BY SURRENDER.

The Surrender did not Establish Freedom—Nor Promote Peace—How the British Public came to Acquiesce in it—The Source of the Error—The Moral—The Boer Response to "Magnanimity"—The Policy of Exclusion—The Destruction of Liberal Principles in South Africa—Not Party Principles, but the Welfare of South Africa Should be the Aim—Let us not say Peace where there is No Peace.. 49

CHAPTER V.

THE NATURAL HISTORY OF REVOLUTION.

The Demand for Reform—Rejected it Becomes Revolution—The Raid—Effect of the Outbreak—The Moral—The New Course—Boer Misgovernment—The Aliens Expulsion Law—Outrages—The Petition to the Queen—Sir Alfred Milner's View of the Situation 67

CHAPTER VI.

BLOEMFONTEIN.

The Bloemfontein Conference—President Kruger's Attitude—Why the Conference was Broken Off—President Kruger's Attitude Still Unchanged—The Actual Situation—The Parting of the Ways 86

CHAPTER VII.

THE STRAIGHTFORWARD POLICY.

Effect of Arousing the Sentiment of Nationality—The Wisdom of the Bloemfontein Programme—The Courses: To the Left—to the Right—and Straight Forward—Difficulties of a Firm Policy—Its Advantages—British Democracy on its Trial .. 101

BRITISH POLICY IN SOUTH AFRICA.

CHAPTER I.

THE PROBLEM.

Democracy and Empire—Duty in the Management of an Empire—Why Great Britain must obtain fair Treatment for the Uitlanders—A Preliminary Survey of the Case—The Unity of South Africa—The Bases of Boer Rights—The Violation of the Spirit of the Compact—Great Britain's Obligations to her own People.

DEMOCRACY AND EMPIRE.

THE task which is set before the British Nation at the present time may be described as the marriage of Democracy with Empire. In the year 1887 a historian, who was then completing his review of the first fifty years of the Queen's reign, gave to the period which he had been studying the title "The Growth of Democracy." He felt, as all men felt who had watched the progress of the Nation's affairs during the long central period of the century, that its characteristic phenomenon was the change in political organisation which had entrusted the Nation's destinies no longer to a class, but to the whole people. That the change was momentous everyone could see, and it was received by many whose training had been completed under the older system with a good deal of misgiving. The electorate had been extended until it could no longer be said to exclude any class of grown men, and the question was, What use would this enlarged electorate make of the power which it had acquired? Before this question could be answered events, in which neither the Government nor the electorate had much share, had shifted the balance of political interest so that men's eyes were directed away from the questions of domestic organisation, which had occupied them during the lifetime of a whole generation, to distant regions of the earth, where pressing business of one sort or another, in which it was evident that the Nation was deeply concerned, had to be transacted. By the time the Queen's reign had completed its sixtieth year the idea uppermost in men's minds was not Democracy, but Empire. Fifty years of legislative change had gradually realised the identity between the people and the nation. Before the people has fully grasped the meaning of the change the nation is rubbing its eyes over the discovery that it has charge of a great Empire, and that, in virtue of the influence inseparable from that charge, it must bear a large share in the responsibility for the general management of the world.

To our fathers the word Empire seemed to have an ominous sound; it was associated with despotic methods of government, and implied possessions and rights. It seemed to be a kind of luxury which could not be dissociated from pride, corruption, and oppression. To-day we are beginning to perceive that for Great Britain, at least, the possession of Empire is an inheritance which cannot be abandoned without suicide, which brings with it a heavy burden of duties, and which places the nation that has it in a stern dilemma. The British Nation must either fit itself by character and by organisation for the fulfilment of those duties, or abdicate its position as a pioneer and a director in the progress of mankind.

Duty in the Management of an Empire.

The present crisis in South Africa is a test of the British Democracy. The course pursued by Great Britain must reveal how far the people are able to rise to the conception of themselves as a Nation, to the idea of a national duty in the management of a specific portion of the Empire, and to the sacrifices, the self-abnegation, without which duty can never be performed. The assertion that Empire, in any sense in which it can be recognised by free men, must be based on self-abnegation may seem at first sight to be a paradox, yet that the paradox is the truth is proved by every page of South African history. The mistakes of the past have almost without exception been due to the attempt to regulate the affairs of one or another South African community according to the theories maintained at the time by one of the political parties in Great Britain, to the neglect of the wishes and feelings of the people primarily concerned, and in contempt of the judgment of the statesmen on the spot, who thought that the needs of the people for whom an arrangement was made were of more importance than the abstract theory which happened for the moment to be popular with professors of political economy in Great Britain and with exponents of political virtue in the House of Commons. It is practically impossible to govern well a far distant country—Australia, Canada, India, or South Africa—according to the theories or the moods of sects or parties in England. The attempt, indeed, has often been made and has invariably had disastrous results: nowhere has it been more persistently repeated, nowhere has it produced such catastrophes, as in the group of Colonies to which public attention has lately been so strongly drawn. Self-abnegation is needed in the management of Colonies to enable the people at home to consider first the needs and the wishes of the Colonists. Self-abnegation is needed also to make efforts of which others than ourselves will reap the benefit. Those who are convinced that at the present time the path of duty lies in prompt and, if necessary, forcible interference with the Oligarchy that governs the Transvaal expect for England no direct or material advantage from such interference. The overthrow of the Boer Oligarchy cannot be replaced by government from the Colonial Office. The Uitlanders who demand their due share in the government of the Transvaal expect and intend in any case to exercise the rights which they claim, and, if it should be necessary for the British arms to make an end of the monopoly of power at present enjoyed by the Boers, the beneficiaries will be, not the people of Great Britain, but the white inhabitants of the Transvaal. There is no new Province to be added to the British dominions, but the elements of civil liberty have to be asserted in a Colony which, so long as the British Nation pursues its Imperial task, must necessarily, both by its geographical situation and by the blood of the greater part of its inhabitants, be amenable to British influence.

Why Great Britain must obtain fair Treatment for the Uitlanders.

The issue which is raised by the refusal of the Boers to treat the Uitlanders as their equals cannot be evaded, and the effects for good or for evil of the conduct of the Uitlanders' case by Great Britain cannot be circumscribed. It is impossible, so long as the British settler in the

Transvaal is a pariah, for the British settler in the Cape Colony to be a respected citizen, the equal of his neighbour of Dutch descent. There can, therefore, be no peace in South Africa until equality has been established from the Zambesi to the Cape. No one can doubt that equality will in the end be asserted, but on the action of Great Britain at this crisis depends the future attitude towards her of other Nations and of her Colonists in Africa and elsewhere. The Uitlanders are for the most part her people, and it is not suggested by any civilised observer that their cause is not just. Great Britain is therefore bound to support their cause and to secure its triumph. If she should fail to do so she would lose the respect of the other civilised Nations, she would dissipate the confidence of all her Colonists, African, Australian, and Canadian, in that purpose which she professes of guarding their interests, upholding their rights, and cherishing their affection; and above all she would have impaired the self-respect of her own people, the only possible basis of national greatness. These are the reasons which justify the belief that the present crisis is above all things a test of the character of the British

Nation at home. The problem is by no means simple, yet the average busy Englishman is imperatively called on to form a correct judgment as to the policy which ought to be pursued. The democratic form of government is, therefore, to be tested. Will it give scope to the nation's best judgment? If that judgment is in favour of intervention, as in all probability it will be, the execution of this decision will involve a considerable effort, great sacrifices, and a sustained determination. Will the democratic system enable the Nation's will to assert itself? Military operations, should they become necessary, may be unusually difficult. Will the democratic system enable the nation to obtain and support administrative efficiency?

In a crisis like this every man must make up his own mind. The attempt will here be made by one whose mind is made up to set plainly before others the elements which go to form the judgment that the Government ought to be supported in the policy of active intervention. It is hoped that a temperate statement of the case may be found worth studying even by those who have hitherto doubted the justice or the expediency of the policy of which Sir Alfred

Milner in South Africa and Mr. Chamberlain at home are the representatives. Perhaps the fair way of proceeding will be to give at once a concise review of the whole case, and of the conclusions to which the reader's assent is asked, reserving a full exposition for later chapters.

A Preliminary Survey of the Case.

The Transvaal is a district about as large as France, inhabited by seven hundred thousand Kaffirs or blacks. Into this district, during a period within the recollection of men now living, a period almost coinciding with the Queen's reign, two hundred and forty-five thousand white men of European descent have migrated. Of these whites sixty-five thousand are Boers, one hundred thousand are of British race, and eighty thousand of other nationalities, European or American. The Boers imagine that they have a proprietary right to the State; that they are the State. They have in their hands the Legislature and the Executive, and they propose to keep both to themselves. So far as the Transvaal is isolated they have the power to do this, for they are armed and the Uitlanders are unarmed. The Uitlanders might overcome them by persuading the natives to join them in a revolt, but are prevented from doing so by the feeling that as against the blacks the white men must stand together.

The Unity of South Africa.

On what does the Boer position rest beyond the fact that being armed they can maintain themselves by force against the Uitlanders and the blacks so long as the Uitlanders and the blacks do not make common cause against them? This mental reservation on the part of the Uitlanders is a point of importance. It implies that there is a community of interest among white men in a country of blacks. The Boer attitude recognises no such community, and would logically drive the Uitlanders to try and employ the blacks on their side. What prevents them is the knowledge that such a course would bring about a war of extermination between whites and blacks all over South Africa. The Boers know this. Their position, therefore, assumes a common white interest, and of this they take advantage to the detriment of the Uitlanders.

At the outset, then, we are met by the fact that the Transvaal is but a part of a larger whole which is South Africa; and that its affairs are not and cannot be treated as though the rest of South Africa did not exist. The presence of a black population as the accompaniment of all the doings of white men forms the bond of a common interest for all the whites in South Africa. The Boer position, then, has not even brute force as its foundation, but only brute force coupled with the assumption that the Uitlanders will recognise a moral obligation not to stir up the blacks against the Boers.

The Bases of Boer Rights.

Turning from force to right, the Boers have to rest their case solely on treaties with Great Britain, on compacts by which Great Britain has recognised a Boer State, and in virtue of which the Boer State is able to make laws. The Transvaal State was recognised as the South African Republic by the Sand River Convention in 1852, which, however, by the proviso against slavery reserved to Great Britain the right of interference in the government of the country.

This Convention was abrogated by the annexation in 1877. In 1881 the Transvaal State was again recognised by the Convention of Pretoria, which accorded self-government "to the inhabitants of the Transvaal territory." This renewal of self-government was a voluntary grant by the Sovereign Power, Great Britain. It was not extorted by force; there had been skirmishes in which small parties of British had been worsted; but the agreement was made just at the moment when the British Army was ready to commence the war in earnest. The motive, the sole motive, ever alleged for the Convention was Mr. Gladstone's belief that the majority of the inhabitants of the Transvaal desired self-government, and had not desired annexation. The Boer State rests solely on the consent of Great Britain to respect the wishes of the majority of the inhabitants. That State thus founded now overrides the majority of its own inhabitants.

The Convention of 1884 by its reservation of a British right to allow or disallow Transvaal Treaties with foreign Powers proves that the State was still considered, and admitted itself to be, under British protection.

The Violation of the Spirit of the Compact.

In 1881, when by the Convention of Pretoria the pre-existing laws were restored, a newcomer who acquired land became a Burgher at once; if he did not acquire land he was required to complete a year's residence and then become a Burgher. In 1882 a law was passed requiring five years' residence and a small fee from newcomers before they could become Burghers. This was the law at the time of the Convention of 1884. Since that time the law has been altered so as to make it practically impossible for any settler to become a Burgher.

The natural consequence of this action would be revolution; the majority would do as the alleged majority did in 1880, they would organise a rebellion and fight for their rights. This is precisely what the people of Johannesburg were considering at the moment when their deliberations were interrupted by Dr. Jameson's Raid, which took them by surprise, and compelled them prematurely to decide either for rebellion or surrender. At the request of the

High Commissioner, who promised that their case should be taken up by the British Government, they gave up their arms. The British Government, indeed, allowed the leaders to be fined and imprisoned, but the recent negotiations were undertaken in fulfilment of the pledge then given by Sir Hercules Robinson.

All the three Conventions contain stipulations by Great Britain on the subject of the black natives. Can it be supposed that Great Britain, while reserving her right to interfere in the Transvaal to secure for the blacks their rights or whatever she might consider fair treatment for them, has no right to interfere to secure fair treatment for whites, the bulk of whom are her own subjects?

This brief preliminary survey shows what the answer must be to the question as to the right. The Boers have taken advantage of Great Britain's inattention to usurp as their exclusive possession the State which was given its self-government in order that the majority of its inhabitants might control its government. They have acted in defiance of right, and Great Britain is entitled to compel them to give up their wrongfully-acquired privileges.

Great Britain's Obligations to her own People.

The second question is whether Great Britain ought to do what she is entitled to do; whether it was worth her while to take up the Uitlanders' case and whether she has any sufficient inducement to carry that case through even if necessary at the sword's point?

The answer is given by a consideration of where the Transvaal is. It is a piece of that South Africa in which a white population lives in the midst of a much larger black population, and where the white population is made up of two races, British and Dutch. The British Government has given equal rights in the Cape and in Natal to both races. In the Transvaal the Boers keep rights to themselves and treat the British with contempt. The antagonism cannot be kept up in the Transvaal without spreading all over South Africa, and if the Englishman counts for nothing in the Transvaal he cannot count at the Cape for a Dutchman's equal, for the South African Colonies are members of one body and the same life-blood circulates through them all. The conflict in the

Transvaal has extended throughout the country. Suppose the British Government fails to put the Uitlanders into their proper place as citizens of the Transvaal. In that case they must take what the Burghers will give them. Great Britain will have abandoned them, and they will abandon her. But they are the same people as the British of the Cape, of Natal, and of Rhodesia. To abandon their case is to alienate all the British in South Africa, and to drive them into the kind of fusion with the Dutch which will lead to a declaration of South African independence.

CHAPTER II.

THE ORIGIN OF SOUTH AFRICA'S TROUBLES.

The use of History to the Statesman—The General Conditions in South Africa—Close of the Reactionary Period—Liberalism and Emancipation—The Backward Policy begins—First Effect: The Great Trek—Why did British Governments go Back?

THE USE OF HISTORY TO THE STATESMAN.

THE history of South Africa has been admirably written by more than one competent hand. Mr. C. P. Lucas, in the fourth volume of his "Historical Geography of the British Colonies," gives a terse and clear review of the facts; Mr. Bryce in his "Impressions of South Africa" gives a historical picture, which is the more valuable because Mr. Bryce is untainted with the modern bias in favour of a strong policy. No one will suspect Mr. Bryce of a disposition to support Mr. Chamberlain or Sir Alfred Milner; yet Mr. Bryce's volume is, perhaps against its author's wish, an unanswerable plea for the cause of the Uitlanders. If history is to be of any assistance to the formation of a political judgment it must be more than a tale that is told, it must be thought over until the true moral has been drawn. But whereas the historian draws a general moral, and usually aims at tracing in his particular story all those varied lessons which it contains, the statesman must ask and answer specific questions. The reader who is trying to judge of the present crisis is trying to be a statesman : he wants to see what the British Government ought to do to-day. The question to which he demands an answer from South African history is : " What mistakes have British Governments made before in South Africa, and how did they come to be made ? " It so happens that the answer in this case is quite clear and quite certain. All the histories tell the same tale ; Mr. Bryce does not care to label " blunder " the mistakes of his own political friends ; Mr. Lucas uses the reserved language of an official. But their readers can never be in doubt as to the errors of the past. Of course, it is impossible to condense into one or two short chapters the whole story of South Africa. There is no need to make the attempt, because the reader can turn to the histories that have been named, and can check by reference to them all the statements that will here be made. But it is necessary to collect into a single view those landmarks of the history by the aid of which a broad view as to the sequence of cause and effect can be reached.

THE GENERAL CONDITIONS IN SOUTH AFRICA.

The fate of European Colonies, so long as they are Colonies, is bound up with the condition of Europe. No Colonial Empire can be kept by a nation unable to hold its place as a Great Power in the European system. At the close of the Eighteenth Century the Dutch had lost their political greatness. From the beginning their State had suffered from the dissensions between the partisans of Democracy and those of Monarchy, and in 1787 the nation that in its great days had resisted the power of Louis XIV. saw its territories overrun and its democratic party put down by a Prussian Army commissioned to support the House of Orange. In 1793 the Revolutionary Government of France declared war at the same time against England and Holland, and the bad management of the Allies enabled the French in the winter of

1794–95 to conquer Holland and to set up in the country a Republic under French protection. Holland was thus in spite of herself ranged among the enemies of England, and her Colonies had to follow the fortunes of war. The Cape was conquered by the British in 1795, but at the Peace of Amiens was given back to the Dutch, who resumed possession in 1803. The war broke out again almost immediately, and in 1805 Pitt sent a small force under Sir David Baird to seize the Cape. In 1806 the Cape was conquered, and at the general peace in 1814, England's legal title to this and other conquered Dutch Colonies was recognised in return for a payment of six millions sterling. The Cape Colonists were the descendants of Dutchmen of the lower classes, whose emigration had taken place during a period of a hundred and fifty years, and of a contingent of Huguenot refugees who had gone out in 1689. They were for the most part peasants (Boers), whose farming had only partially adapted itself to their new surroundings; they were tenacious of their evangelical religion and of its bigotry, and held slaves whose numbers slightly exceeded their own. Isolation from the civilised world and contact with the Bushmen, the Hottentots, and the Kaffirs had prevented their progress in arts and manners. In 1820 a batch of British emigrants were exported to the Cape, and some four thousand of them settled at Bathurst, near Algoa Bay. That was the beginning of a gradual influx of British settlers, which, however, has never assumed such proportions as to make the British in the Cape Colony as numerous as the people of Dutch descent. On the eve of the British occupation (1805) the European population of the Colony was about twenty-six thousand. In 1891 the European population of all the South African Colonies was seven hundred and sixty thousand. This expansion took place in conditions peculiar to South Africa and distinguishing its history from that of other European Colonies of recent growth. The Europeans, who from the Cape have spread themselves to the North as far as the Zambesi, and to the East as far as the Indian Ocean, have not occupied an uninhabited country and have not driven out the dark tribes whom they have met. The first white settlers at the Cape found the country inhabited by Bushmen, Hottentots and Kaffirs. There was no war of extermination, though the whites asserted their mastery. But the rise of the European Colonies has been contemporaneous with a great inrush of Kaffir tribes, which have come from the more Northerly regions, and have swept over the country in a series of waves, exterminating or conquering their dark-skinned predecessors and setting up each in turn or each in the district to which design or circumstances brought it a barbarous military despotism. These Kaffir systems have had to be one after another overthrown; the tribes have, however, not been destroyed; they have been defeated and disarmed, and the tribesmen continue in every district to form the bulk of the population. Three quarters of a million whites are dispersed among three and a quarter millions of blacks. There are here two facts which must never be allowed to leave the mind: the first, that all the actions of the whites take place in an environment of blacks; and the second, that the expansive efforts of the Colonists were accompanied by an aggressive movement of the Kaffir tribes not caused by any action of the white settlers. This Kaffir migration Southwards could not be foreseen nor its nature understood until its course was run. It was a factor which the Statesmen of the middle of the century can hardly be blamed for not appreciating; but in forming a judgment now on the course of South African development it must be steadily kept in view.

Close of the Reactionary Period.

The Dutch Colonists had not been happy in their relations with their Chartered Company nor with the Government of the States General which had succeeded it. The British Government assumed control in the period of reaction, of which Castlereagh was in his day the type, and the early English Governors were as despotic as their Dutch predecessors. They were at first not much interfered with from home; but between 1820 and 1830 the British Government began its experiments in governing the Cape. There was a rearrangement of Local Governments and of the Law Courts, perhaps good in itself, but eminently distasteful to the Dutch, and in 1827 the decree went forth that English should be the official language. At that time not more than one Colonist in seven was British, so that one wonders whether the wise men in Downing Street ever asked themselves what language the Colonists spoke.

Liberalism and Emancipation.

About 1830 the pendulum in Great Britain began to swing back again. There had been during the long war and after it too much repression. For many a long year the ideal now became to be to have as little government as possible. This general theory covered many noble purposes, and a profound attachment to the idea of freedom and humanity. One of the humane objects of the time was the abolition of slavery, and in 1834 the legislation by which slavery was abolished in British territories came into force. The law was right and just in principle, but its application caused no little hardship in detail. The Cape Colonists resented it partly because the change pressed heavily on them, and still more because they themselves had not been converted to the new view. The slave-owners were compensated; but those at the Cape received only a million and a quarter for slaves valued by the Commissioners at three millions sterling. The Government is not to be blamed for carrying through the emancipation of the slaves, nor perhaps for the sufferings which it involved to many of the owners. Nor can any Government be held responsible for the action of the missionaries, who set to work about this time in South Africa and became for many years the censors of the Dutch. The missionaries saw black men in the light of the Kingdom of Heaven as potential angels or saints. They therefore resented the practical treatment of the blacks as inferior beings, and the standard of humanity which they set up was an offence and a stumbling-block to the Dutch Boers.

The Backward Policy Begins.

In 1834 Sir Benjamin D'Urban, being Governor of the Cape, and the Eastern boundary of the Colony being the Keiskamma, 12,000 Kaffirs crossed that border and invaded the settlements, killing, burning, and destroying. The raid was repulsed and the border crossed in a counter attack by the British. After the thorough defeat of the Kaffirs the Governor proclaimed the annexation of the country beyond the Keiskamma as far as the Kei. But the British Government ordered the new Province to be restored to the Kaffirs and moved the frontier back to the Keiskamma. Why did the Government do this? Solely because they were bitten by a theory that the Empire was too big and ought not to be extended. They made no attempt to study the local conditions; their notion of government was to carry out a theory. The Governor, in a despatch to the Colonial Secretary, summed up the case in the words: "Your Lordship in England and I upon the spot have seen all these African matters under different views." That sentence is in a nutshell the history of the course of British Governments in dealing with South Africa. The man on the spot sees the needs of the situation. The Government at home has its head full of theory, either that the Empire is too big or that it is too little. The man on the spot is overruled, and twenty years afterwards the measure he was trying to carry out is seen, too late, to have been necessary.

First Effect: The Great Trek.

The backward move of 1835 was too much for the Dutch Boers. The Government had disturbed their customs, forced a foreign language on them, taken away their slaves, forbidden them to treat the blacks as inferior beings, and at last restored a conquered Province to the Kaffirs. Thousands of Boers emigrated. They set out with their families on waggons drawn by oxen and moved off into the interior. Some went to the district between the Orange and the Vaal Rivers, now the Orange Free State; others went beyond the mountains into what is now Natal; others again went into the country north of the Vaal River, since called the Transvaal. The British Government was working on its theory that the Empire was too big, which at bottom was nothing but an excuse for indolence; the Ministers would not take the trouble to study the fringe of the Empire, and preferred to cut it off. But the Government's servants on the spot knew better, and, as far as they were allowed, did their duty. An Act of Parliament of 1836 had applied the Criminal Law of the Cape Colony to all the territory South of the 25th degree of latitude. But when, in 1842, a Colonial Judge proclaimed British Sovereignty up to that limit, the Government annulled the proclamation, while at the same time claiming the white men within the limit as British subjects. In 1834 Governor D'Urban sent home a petition from the British settlers at Port Natal, which place had been granted in 1824 by a native chief to Lieutenant Farewell, praying for the formation there of a Government establishment. The request was refused. When the Boers began to come into Natal the Cape Government sent a garrison to Port Natal. The Home Government declined to annex the place and the garrison had to be recalled. But when the Boers of Natal attacked the Zulus, and the Zulus asked for British protection—when at the same time a Dutch and an American ship appeared off the coast and there was a chance of interference by Holland or by the United States, and when also the Boers and the British had come to blows in the district—the Government at last annexed Natal. Can it be a matter of wonder that these Boers acquired a hatred of the British Government and all its ways? The greater part of them withdrew beyond the mountains into the country North and South of the Vaal. In 1848 the Boer Leader, Pretorius, wrote to the Governor of the Cape: "Are we worse, are we more contemptible than the coloured population? To them are acknowledged and secured the lands they have inherited; to them are allowed the privileges of self-government and their own laws, but as soon as we whites are on the same lands, which we have justly obtained from them, these privileges are immediately taken from us." The discontent was not yet too great to be overcome by a straightforward policy. In 1848 Sir Harry Smith proclaimed British sovereignty over the district between the Vaal and the Orange Rivers, and appointed a British Resident. The Boers flew to arms. Sir Harry Smith defeated them at Boomplatz, and the annexation was carried through; fresh European settlers came in, and there was every prospect of prosperity. The settlers asked for representative government, but were denied it, and in 1852 the Government's policy was declared to be the "ultimate abandonment of the Orange River Sovereignty." In the same year the new backward policy was applied to the region further to the North and embodied in the Sand River Convention, by which "the emigrant farmers beyond the Vaal River" were given the right to manage their own affairs, subject to the condition that they should neither permit nor practise slavery. The Boers of the Orange River Territory wanted self-government, but not independence; they were ready to keep their allegiance to the Queen. There was about this time in the neighbourhood of the Orange River Territory a rising of the Basutos, against whom the Cape Governor fought a battle in which his success was doubtful, though the Basutos afterwards came to terms with him. To retain the country would be troublesome, for troops would be needed to overawe the Basutos. Accordingly, in 1854, Sir Harry Smith's annexation of 1848 was undone, the British sovereignty renounced, and the inhabitants obliged, by the Bloemfontein Convention, to constitute the Orange Free State as a Republic.

Why did British Governments go Back?

It is now the reader's turn to work. If he does not care to make up his mind about the course of past Government action in South Africa up to 1854 he had better get rid of his vote and consider himself an Uitlander in his own country. A citizen's business is to make up his mind about these things, so that his influence in future national decisions will go to prevent the repetition of old mistakes.

The Government was evidently wrong in its notion that the Empire was too big; in spite of all its efforts the Empire kept on expanding. It was evidently a mistake of the Cabinets to suppose that they knew better in London how to manage South Africa than did the men who were on the spot in charge of the Cape Colony.

But why did the Governments one after another make these mistakes? They were educated men, and had read Roman history; why did they not copy the Romans, and steadfastly refuse to have any going back? Two answers may be suggested, and the reader must grapple for himself with the problem whether either of them is right. In the first place, the Ministers were under the influence of the dominant opinions of the time, which took shape from the Party conflicts of that epoch. The battle of the extension of the suffrage was waging at home. Those who favoured Reform as it was called developed a theory of representative government which absorbed their whole attention. The word of the period was "the people," and the aim was to give the people rights. The forgotten word was "the Nation," and little was said of duty. We are out of that period now and can take a wider view. We know as the lesson of three thousand years that a nation implies government, the indispensable condition of a satisfactory human life. Government, like charity, begins at home; like charity, when genuine, it does not stay at home, but goes out into the world as its own missionary. Every great nation tries to take its part in governing the world, and the test of a nation's greatness is partly the excellence of its practice in governing, and partly the success with which it extends that practice beyond its own original borders. These ideas were forgotten in the period of conflict over Reform. The Nation was divided against itself, and its action in the world was therefore fitful and irresolute.

A second explanation is also worth considering. There was no one responsible for what was done. The British Government is, as Lord Rosebery has well said, carried on by a Secret Committee; and, as Lord Rosebery has not said, no man of that Committee can by the Constitution be called to account for his acts. If there is a mistake followed by general indignation the Committee can be cashiered and sent for a time to sit on the Opposition benches. The system seems to give satisfaction, but it does not lead to the formation of strong characters ready to wield authority and to identify themselves with their acts even to the point of risking their own personal ruin.

CHAPTER III.

1877–1881: ORDERS, COUNTER-ORDERS, DISORDERS.

Lord Carnarvon's Policy—Backwards Once More—Why the Transvaal was Annexed—Mr. Gladstone in Opposition—Mr. Gladstone in Office—The Surrender—The Loyal Inhabitants—Mr. Gladstone's Pledge—The Fulfilment.

IN 1854 Sir George Grey became Governor of the Cape. After some experience he came to the conclusion that, though there had been great mistakes in the management of South Africa, it was still possible to remedy them.

"In their hurry to be rid of trouble, responsibility, and expenditure, the Imperial Government had conceded territories and alienated subjects without waiting to ascertain the true wishes of the people, and before any free form of government had been introduced into or tried in any part of South Africa. Based on misconception, the policy had failed, resulting in weak unstable European communities, and in widespread and dangerous ill-feeling on the part of the natives. For a remedy he looked to a Federal Union, in which the separate Colonies and States, each with its own local Government and Legislature, should be combined under a general representative Legislature led by a responsible Ministry, specially charged with the duty of providing for common defence." (Lucas, p. 261.)

At this time the Burghers of the Orange Free State desired Federal Union, and the Volksraad resolved that "a union of alliance with the Cape Colony either on the plan of federation or otherwise is desirable." The only result was that the British Government decided that British sovereignty over the Orange Free State should not be resumed, and that Sir George Grey was recalled. He was afterwards sent back, however, but not allowed to carry out the wise policy which he had proposed.

Lord Carnarvon's Policy.

In 1874 Mr. Disraeli became Prime Minister with a strong majority behind him, and he appointed Lord Carnarvon to be Colonial Secretary. In 1877 Lord Carnarvon carried through Parliament a Permissive Confederation Act authorising the creation of a Federal Union between such South African colonies as should be willing to join. At the same time he selected Sir Bartle Frere as Governor and High Commissioner to carry the scheme into effect. When Sir Bartle Frere had been a few days at the Cape he learnt that British sovereignty had just been proclaimed by Sir Theophilus Shepstone over the Transvaal Republic. Sir Theophilus Shepstone had been sent out as High Commissioner to inquire into the condition of the Transvaal, and was empowered, in case it should seem to him necessary, and provided he was satisfied that a sufficient number of the inhabitants desired to become British subjects, to annex the country, and to take over its administration. The annexation was undertaken, not on the ground that the majority of the Boers wished it—there is no possibility now of proving that at the time the majority was not ready to acquiesce—but partly because the country was in a state of anarchy, and because the many British residents there were in constant fear of their lives and appealed to the Queen's Government for protection, and partly because the Transvaal could not defend itself against the Kaffirs of Sekukuni and against the Zulus.

Backwards Once More.

After the annexation there was the usual mismanagement. Lord Carnarvon disappeared from the Government. The promises which Sir

Theophilus Shepstone with his authority had made of representative institutions were not fulfilled. Sir Theophilus Shepstone was recalled and the country subjected to a military despotism which in fact misgoverned, and which exasperated the Boers. At the same time Mr. Gladstone in England made himself the one-sided advocate of the Boer case. The British Government broke the power first of the Zulus, and then of Sekukuni. Mr. Gladstone, when he returned to office with a great majority, refused to cancel the annexation, but when the Boers took up arms, when they had had a number of minor successes, when the British forces had not yet seriously begun the war, he suddenly gave way and annulled all that had been done by Lord Carnarvon.

Why the Transvaal was Annexed.

It would be hard to give a fairer and more impartial judgment on the annexation of the Transvaal than that of Mr. Bryce.

"The Transvaal Republic was bankrupt and helpless, distracted by internal quarrels, unable to collect any taxes, apparently unable to defend itself against its Kaffir enemies, and likely to be the cause of native troubles which might probably spread till they affected all Europeans in South Africa. There was some reason to believe that the citizens, though they had not been consulted, would soon acquiesce in the change, especially when they found, as they soon did find, that the value of property rose with the prospect of security, and of the carrying out of internal improvements by a strong and wealthy Power. Such was certainly the belief of Sir T. Shepstone and of Lord Carnarvon, and it seemed to be confirmed by the apparent tranquillity which the Boers exhibited. So indeed they might have acquiesced, notwithstanding their strong love of independence, had they been wisely dealt with. But the British Government proceeded forthwith to commit three capital blunders." ("Impressions of South Africa," p. 195.)

The three blunders enumerated by Mr. Bryce were, first, the failure to grant the local autonomy which was promised at the time of annexation; secondly, the maladministration of Sir Owen Lanyon; and thirdly, the defeat by the British of the Zulus and of Sekukuni. The destruction of the Zulu power and the reduction of Sekukuni's strongholds ought not to be called a blunder, for it was a necessity, but it certainly had the effect of relieving the Boers from an apprehension which was grave enough to reconcile them to Lord Carnarvon's policy.

Mr. Gladstone in Opposition.

In November and December, 1879, Mr. Gladstone delivered a series of political speeches in the South of Scotland. They were attacks on the Government, and it is important that the reader of to-day should realise the tone in which he spoke.

At Edinburgh he said of the Government:

"They have annexed in Africa the Transvaal territory, inhabited by a free European, Christian, Republican community, which they have thought proper to bring within the limits of a Monarchy, although out of eight thousand persons in that Republic qualified to vote upon the subject we are told—and I have never seen the statement officially contradicted—that six thousand five hundred protested against it. These are the circumstances under which we undertake to transform Republicans into subjects of a Monarchy. We have made war on the Zulus. We have thereby become responsible for their territory; and not only this, but we are now, as it appears from the latest advices, about to make war upon a chief lying to the northward of the Zulus; and Sir Bartle Frere, who was the great authority for the proceedings of the Government in Afghanistan, has announced in South Africa that it will be necessary for us to extend our dominions until we reach the Portuguese frontier to the North. So much for Africa."

At Dalkeith he said:

"If we cast our eyes to South Africa, what do we behold? That a Nation whom we term savages have, in defence of their own land, offered their naked bodies to the terribly improved artillery and arms of modern European science, and have been mowed down by hundreds and by thousands, having committed no offence, but having, with rude and ignorant courage, done what were for them, and done faithfully and bravely, what were for them the duties of patriotism. You may talk of glory, you may offer rewards—and you are right to give rewards to the gallantry of your soldiers, who I think are entitled not only to our admiration for courage, but to our compassion for the nature of the duties they have been called to perform—but the grief and pain none the less remain."

At Glasgow he said:

"In Africa you have before you the memory of bloodshed, of military disaster, the record of ten thousand Zulus—such is the computation of Bishop Colenso—slain for no other offence than their attempt to defend against your artillery with their naked bodies their hearths and homes, their wives and families. You have the invasion of a free people in the Transvaal, and you have, I fear, in one quarter or another—I will not enter into details, which might be injurious to the public interest—prospects of further disturbance and shedding of blood."

Mr. Gladstone's speeches were widely circulated among the Boers, who believed that if returned to power Mr. Gladstone would bring about the restoration of their independence. They sent Messrs. Kruger and Joubert as a Deputation to the Cape, and these two gentlemen persuaded the Cape Parliament to reject the confederation scheme, which was at that time submitted to it by Sir Bartle Frere.

Mr. Gladstone in Office.

As soon as Mr. Gladstone was once more Prime Minister he found himself compelled to abandon the tone of his Midlothian speeches. In the debate on the Queen's Speech he said:

"I do not know whether there is an absolute union of opinion on this side of the House as to the policy in which the assumption of the Transvaal originated. Undoubtedly, as far as I am myself concerned, I did not approve of that assumption. I took no part in questioning it nor in the attempt to condemn it, because, in my opinion, whether the assumption was wise or unwise, it having been done, no good but only mischief was to be done by the intervention of this House. But whatever our original opinions were on that policy—and the opinions of the majority of those who sit on this side of the House were decidedly adverse to it—we had to confront a state of facts, and the main fact which met us was the existence of the large native population in the Transvaal, to whom, by the establishment of the Queen's supremacy, we hold ourselves to have given a pledge. That is the acceptance of facts, and that is the sense in which my right hon. friend, and all those who sit with him, may, if they think fit, say we accept the principles on which the late Government proceeded. It is quite possible to accept the consequences of a policy, and yet to retain the original difference of opinion with regard to the character of that policy as long as it was a matter of discussion."

And shortly after he wrote to Messrs. Kruger and Joubert saying:

"It is undoubtedly matter for much regret that it should since the annexation have appeared that so large a number of the population of Dutch origin in the Transvaal are opposed to the annexation of that territory, but it is impossible to consider that question as if it were presented for the first time. We have to deal with a state of things which has existed for a considerable period, during which obligations have been contracted, especially, though not exclusively, towards the native population, which cannot be set aside.

"Looking to all the circumstances, both of the Transvaal and the rest of South Africa, and to the necessity of preventing a renewal of disorders which might lead to disastrous consequences, not only to the Transvaal, but to the whole of South Africa, our judgment is that the Queen cannot be advised to relinquish her sovereignty over the Transvaal, but, consistently with the maintenance of that sovereignty, we desire that the white inhabitants of the Transvaal should, without prejudice to the rest of the population, enjoy the fullest liberty to manage their local affairs. We believe that this liberty may be most easily and promptly conceded to the Transvaal as a member of a South African Confederation."

The Surrender.

No attempt had been made to give representative institutions to the Transvaal. Sir Garnet Wolseley in 1879 had set up the government of a Crown Colony, with a nominated Executive Council and Legislative Assembly. So as soon, therefore, as the Boers were satisfied that Mr. Gladstone would not fulfil the hopes which, when in Opposition, he had raised, they prepared their revolt, and on the 16th of December, 1880, a proclamation was issued declaring the Republic to be re-established under the provisional leadership of Messrs. Kruger, Pretorius, and Joubert. At that time there were a few detachments of British troops scattered in small garrisons over the country. One of these parties of two hundred and sixty men was attacked by a large number of Boers at Bronker's Spruit on the 20th of December, and after a loss of one hundred and fifty-seven killed and wounded, surrendered. The other parties were surrounded and besieged. Sir George Colley, the General in command in Natal, collected the troops available in that Colony, and marched towards the Transvaal to attempt the relief of the garrisons. He found the Boers posted in a strong position at Lang's Nek, and on the 28th of January, 1881, he attacked them with only one thousand four hundred men. He was repulsed, and a few days later had a second fight, also unsuccessful, though on a smaller scale, at Ingogo. On the night of February 22nd he marched with four hundred men to the top of Majuba Hill, which dominated Lang's Nek. Next day the Boer sharpshooters, finding that the party on the hill was unsupported and without artillery, attacked the position. The defence was not well conducted; the British troops were badly beaten, and Sir George Colley was killed at the crisis of the fight. Reinforcements had already begun to reach Natal, and Sir Evelyn Wood, who succeeded Sir George Colley in the command, was very soon at the head of a force sufficient to crush the Boers. But on March 5th the Government at home ordered an armistice to be concluded. This was negotiated on the 6th, and in less than three weeks, without any further fighting, terms of peace involving the restoration of self-government to the Transvaal were agreed on. On August 3rd was signed at

Pretoria the Convention by which "complete self-government, subject to the suzerainty of Her Majesty, her heirs, and successors," was to be "accorded to the inhabitants of the Transvaal territory."

THE LOYAL INHABITANTS.

In May, 1881, while the negotiations were in progress, a petition was sent to the House of Commons by the loyal inhabitants of the Transvaal. A few passages from that petition deserve to be recalled to-day :—

"That your petitioners believe that the annexation was acquiesced in by a majority of the inhabitants, and was looked upon as an act calculated to create confidence and credit in the country, a belief which is borne out by the fact that almost all the old officials appointed by the former Government, or elected by the people, remained in office under the new Government; and your petitioners further believe, that if the promises expressed and implied in the annexation proclamation had been carried out fully in the spirit of the Proclamation, the whole of the inhabitants would, in time, have become loyal subjects of Her Majesty.

"That the annexation was followed by an immediate accession of confidence, and it marked the commencement of an era of progress and advancement, which has steadily increased up to the present time, despite the numerous drawbacks and disadvantages to which the country has been subjected, and some of which have been the result of Imperial action.

"That, notwithstanding the promises expressed and implied in the annexation Proclamation, the country has been governed as a Crown Colony, and no opportunity has been afforded to the inhabitants of controlling the policy which has regulated its administration, and your petitioners are in no way responsible for the late lamentable war, or for the disgraceful peace which has concluded it.

* * * * *

"That the value of property increased at least threefold during the English occupation, and that the increase progressed in a ratio correspondent with the reliance placed on the promises of English officials. Indeed, some of your petitioners are prepared to state, on oath if required, that they invested money immediately after or in direct consequence of a statement made by a Governor of the Transvaal or a Minister of the British Crown.

"That the towns are almost exclusively inhabited by loyal subjects, and English farmers and traders are scattered all over the country.

* * * * *

"That most of the loyal inhabitants intend to realise their property, even at a sacrifice, and to leave the country, but that those who are compelled by force of circumstances to remain in it will be deprived of the protection and security afforded by English rule, and they respectfully submit they have a right to ask that the fullest and most substantial pledges be exacted from the contemplated Boer Government for their safety, and for the exercise of their privileges as British subjects."

Mr. Gladstone's Pledge.

At the beginning of June Mr. Gladstone wrote a letter to the loyal inhabitants, in which he said :

"Her Majesty's Government willingly and thankfully acknowledge the loyal co-operation which Her Majesty's Forces received at Pretoria and elsewhere by the inhabitants, and we sympathise with the privations and sufferings which they endured. I must, however, observe that so great was the preponderance of the Boers who rose in arms against the Queen's authority, that the whole country, except the posts occupied by the British troops, fell at once practically into their hands. Again, the memorialists themselves only estimate the proportion of settlers not Transvaal Boers at one-seventh. Nearly, though not quite, the whole of the Boers have appeared to be united in sentiment; and Her Majesty's Government could not deem it their duty to set aside the will of so large a majority by the only possible means, namely, the permanent maintenance of a powerful military force in the country. Such a course would have been inconsistent alike with the spirit of the Treaty of 1852, with the grounds on which the annexation was sanctioned, and with the general interests of South Africa, which especially require that harmony should prevail between the white races.

"On the other hand, in the settlement which is now in progress, every care will be taken to secure to the settlers, of whatever origin, the full enjoyment of their property and of all civil rights."

The Fulfilment.

The pledges conveyed in the last sentence received such fulfilment as they were to have by the insertion in the Convention of the following clauses:

"Article XII.—All persons holding property in the said State on the 8th day of August, 1881, will continue to enjoy the rights of property which they have enjoyed since the annexation. No person who has remained loyal to Her Majesty during the recent hostilities shall suffer any molestation by reason of his loyalty or be liable to any criminal prosecution or civil action for any part taken in connection with such hostilities; and all such persons will have full liberty to reside in the country, with enjoyment of all civil rights and protection for their persons and property."

"Article XXVI.—All persons other than natives conforming themselves to the laws of the Transvaal State (a) will have full liberty with their families to enter, travel, or reside in any part of the Transvaal State; (b) they will be entitled to hire or possess houses, manufactories, warehouses, shops, and premises; (c) they may carry on their commerce either in person or by any agents whom they may think fit to employ; (d) they will not be subject in respect of their persons or property, or in respect of their commerce or industry, to any taxes, whether general or local, other than those which are or may be imposed upon Transvaal citizens."

The Articles were repeated in the Convention of 1884.

CHAPTER IV.

PEACE BY SURRENDER.

The Surrender did not Establish Freedom—Nor Promote Peace—How the British Public Came to Acquiesce in it—The Source of the Error—The Moral—The Boer Response to "Magnanimity"—The Policy of Exclusion—The Destruction of Liberal Principles in South Africa—Not Party Principles, but the Welfare of South Africa Should be the Aim—Let us not say Peace where there is No Peace.

It is absolutely necessary that we should make up our minds whether Mr. Gladstone in giving up the Transvaal in 1881 did right or wrong. Such opposition as there is to the policy of which Sir Alfred Milner is the exponent has its roots in the belief, which still lingers in many minds, that there was something noble about the policy of 1881, and that it was the legitimate outcome of Liberal principles, which ought not now to be abandoned. That policy has been defended on two grounds: First, that a free Nation is bound to recognise the principles of freedom even when they tell against itself;

and second, that if the war had been fought out there would have been civil war throughout South Africa, accompanied by an embitterment of feeling which would have destroyed the peace and welfare of the two Colonies for many years. Neither of these defences will bear the light of day.

The Surrender did not Establish Freedom.

The Convention of Pretoria professed in its preamble to guarantee self-government to the inhabitants of the Transvaal territory. If this had been done no fault could be found with Mr. Gladstone. The one cure for all the troubles was then, and is now, the establishment of self-government for the inhabitants of the country. Self-government, in the sense in which alone it can be described as a principle that Great Britain ought to recognise, means representative government, the kind of government which has grown up in Great Britain, and has been given by her to all her great Colonies; the system which secures to all classes their share in making the laws which they obey, and in choosing and criticising the Executive which is to administer them. But this kind of government was not given to the Transvaal: the Fourth Article of the Convention stipulated that the government of the Transvaal State should be handed over to Messrs. Kruger, Pretorius, and Joubert, "who will forthwith cause a Volksraad to be elected and convened, and the Volksraad thus elected and convened will decide as to the further administration of the government of the said State." The three men named were the three Leaders of the Party of Revolt. It was taken for granted that they represented the inhabitants of the country; the British settlers and the loyal Boers were ignored; no guarantee whatever was taken for the establishment of what throughout the British world is known as representative government. The clauses inserted in the Convention for the protection of British residents show clearly enough that Mr. Gladstone, so far from intending to establish freedom, simply intended to surrender the country to the rebellious Party among the Boers. Freedom could have been established only by the fulfilment of Lord Carnarvon's policy, by the assertion of British authority, and the establishment under that authority of institutions representative of all the white inhabitants. These had been promised in the name of the Government by Sir Theophilus Shepstone, and the breach of that promise constituted the true departure from British or from Liberal principles.

Nor Promote Peace.

The second defence is a mere excuse. Had Sir Evelyn Wood been instructed to use his forces energetically for the re-establishment of the Queen's authority, there would no doubt have been for a time discontent in the Orange Free State and at the Cape; but in proportion to the honesty and the efficiency of the Government set up in the Transvaal would have been the speed with which the bitterness would have passed away. The surrender did not produce either peace or harmony; on the contrary, it exasperated the British, and embittered the Dutch throughout the country. The Boers were not satisfied. They did not honestly accept either the suzerainty of the Queen or the frontiers assigned to their State; so far from believing that they had been treated with magnanimity they regarded themselves as the conquerors of the British, and cherished the memory of the skirmishes of their revolt as battles in a war of independence.

How the British Public came to Acquiesce in it.

The most surprising feature in all this strange eventful history is that the people of Great Britain acquiesced in the surrender. That fact gives pause to many who would otherwise unhesitatingly give judgment against Mr. Gladstone. But the explanation is not far to seek. There had been a widespread reaction against Lord Beaconsfield's policy, due less to the nature of the policy than to the way in which it had been presented to the Nation. The country had been divided as to the Eastern policy of the Conservative Cabinet, and the expression "coffee-house babble" with which Lord Beaconsfield had dismissed the first reports, afterwards more than confirmed, of painful events in Bulgaria, had fired the indignation of thousands of men, who as a rule took little interest in foreign affairs. Mr. Gladstone had returned to public life and to the platform to place himself on the crest of this wave of feeling. He had attacked the Government's policy at all points; its management had not been altogether fortunate, and Mr. Gladstone, by denouncing alike the policy pursued in the East, in Afghanistan, in Zululand, and in the Transvaal, produced a flood of generous sentiment which carried him into office. Those who had voted on his side were committed to him and ready to accept even defective parts of a case with which they were in general sympathy. He was able to persuade his followers, who were too glad to believe that the retrocession of the Transvaal was an act of supreme magnanimity. But of those who then were half convinced on this point how many can now retain their belief? Mr. Gladstone in his Midlothian Campaign used language which, while it ignored the reasons for the annexation, encouraged the Boers and made his followers sympathise with the Boers against Great Britain. When he became Minister he shuffled out of his previous position and announced his resolve to abide by the annexation. Not until after the repulses with which the war opened did he discover that it would be magnanimous to concede without first asserting the honour of the British arms.

If Mr. Gladstone was right the Dutch at the Cape, where they outnumber the British, are entitled to revolt and to declare the Cape Colony a Boer Republic, and Great Britain ought to recognise their independence and to compel the loyal Cape Dutch and British to become foreigners or Uitlanders in their own country. That is, indeed, the policy of the Afrikander Bond, of which Mr. Gladstone was the spiritual father.

The Source of the Error.

Mr. Gladstone's mistake was a repetition of that of 1835 and of 1854. He left South Africa out of his calculations. He was thinking of how to deal with Parties at home, and of his theory that the Empire was too big, instead of studying the needs of South Africa. He overruled, as though it were of no account, the judgment of all the men whose knowledge of that country ought to have been his guide.

The Moral.

The lesson of the events of 1877–1881 is that the causes of the mistakes then made should in future be avoided. The root of all the error was in ignoring the facts of South Africa. The Governments at home looked at their pet theory—the Empire too big—and at the tone which would bring applause in public meetings of voters who could not at the time check the statements of the speakers by a full knowledge of the South African facts. The right way would have been to have supported the men on the spot—Sir Benjamin D'Urban, Sir Harry Smith, Sir George Grey, Sir Theophilus Shepstone. This holds good at the present moment. Sir Alfred Milner is as able, as judicial, as high-minded as any of his predecessors. His command of the facts of the case is admitted by all Parties. The nation will hardly go wrong in supporting him.

From 1835 to 1884 the pet theory, of which the reign was interrupted only between 1874 and 1880, was that the Empire was too big and ought to be cut down. This theory did infinite harm. The moral for to-day is not that the theory should be reversed and that we should declare the Empire too little, which would lead to follies as great as those of the past, but that we should ask our Governments to leave theories alone and to attend to their business, to the good management of the Empire as it is, regulating the affairs of each portion of it in accordance with the actual local needs.

The Boer Response to "Magnanimity."

The Boers, as has been said, resented the reservation of British suzerainty, and in 1884 Mr. Gladstone consented to a new Convention, in which the title "the South African Republic" was used, and which contains a stipulation that the Republic "will conclude no Treaty or engagement with any state or nation other than the Orange Free State, nor with any native tribe to the eastward or westward of the Republic until the same has been approved by Her Majesty the Queen." The Boers seem never to have had any intention to be bound by the Conventions. They persisted in an aggressive foreign policy: between 1882 and 1884 a number of them crossed the frontier into Zululand, and by siding with one party among the natives established their authority over a district which was called "The New Republic," and which was annexed to the Transvaal in 1888. An attempt was made in like manner to secure for the Transvaal the districts of Stellaland and Vryburg beyond its western frontier, so that at the close of 1884 it became necessary for the protection of these districts to send Sir Charles Warren with a military force to take them under British protection.

The Policy of Exclusion.

About 1882 the discovery of goldfields in the Transvaal brought about a rapid influx of European immigrants, first to Barberton, and three or four years later to the Witwatersrand. Then began to be seen the effect of Mr. Gladstone's supposed assertion of the principles of freedom. The discovery of goldfields is not a new experience in modern history. It has always brought with it a great inrush of miners and speculators, of whom no doubt a percentage are mere temporary visitors, but of whom a large number take up their permanent abode in the region where they have found work and wealth. In California and in Australia these in-comers have been a source of strength to the country, for it has been as a rule a matter of course that they should speedily acquire the citizenship of the State in which they have settled and become attached, as Colonists usually become attached, to the country of their choice. The Boers, as has been seen, had no intention of attracting further citizens. Their one object was to keep in their own hands the power which they had acquired, and as early as 1882 the Volksraad passed a law imposing on candidates for the franchise a residence of five years, to be accompanied by registry on the Field Cornet's books, and a payment of £25 on admission to the rights of citizenship. This was before the mining epoch. By 1890 the tide of immigration had brought in a large population of new settlers. The Boers were resolved that these new-comers should for ever remain foreigners, though it was evident that the bulk of them intended to make the Transvaal their permanent home. Accordingly an Act was passed by which no person not already a burgher, or the son of a burgher, could acquire the full franchise in less than fourteen years, or before the age of forty. During all the fourteen years the new-comer must renounce his rights in his old country, and take on himself the obligations without the rights of a subject of the Transvaal, but the law gave him at the end of the fourteen years no right to citizenship, but merely the right to ask for it from the Volksraad, which was at liberty to reject the request. The object of this law has never been doubted; it was to retain the Government of the Transvaal in the hands of the original Boers and of their families, to the perpetual exclusion of new-comers, who were to be left either as resident aliens, the subjects of a distant Government, or as a subordinate class of unenfranchised subjects occupying a position midway between that of the Boer Burgher and that of the Kaffir.

The Destruction of Liberal Principles in South Africa.

It is evident that the Boers could pass in their Volksraad whatever laws they pleased, but it is equally evident that the law just described was in fact as well as in intention a gross injustice. A large number of the immigrants necessarily became permanent inhabitants of the Transvaal; their work and the growth of their families were sure to root them to the soil, and they formed a considerable portion of the white population of the country; they were therefore entitled, not indeed by the laws of the Transvaal, but by the laws of human nature, to the fair and efficient administration of general and of local government, as well as to the consideration of their interests in legislation. In the modern State the only guarantee that a class of persons shall have these benefits consists in their due representation in the Legislature and in the body which appoints and controls the executive. This is an elementary principle of freedom; it is the essence of what used to be called Liberal principles. Thus Mr. Gladstone's action in 1881 was a fatal blow to the spread in South Africa of the traditional principles of his Party; it placed the most serious obstacles in the way of the growth of Democracy in that part of the world, where, in fact, it introduced an Oligarchy of the lowest type. For in the Transvaal political power has since 1881 been the monopoly of a caste of peasants, uneducated and bigotted, whose original trek into the wilderness was a secession for the purpose of founding what was intended to be in spirit, if not in the letter, a slave-holding State. This Oligarchy is now engaged in the effort to exclude from all political influence a class of men more numerous and better educated than itself, many of them trained in the working of free institutions, a class which has in a few years by its enterprise, energy, and intelligence enriched the country. Yet the Oligarchy, the ruling caste, has so little of the aristocratic character that its Government extorts from the unenfranchised inhabitants a vast revenue, which has become a fountain of corruption to the ruling caste. There was an old Liberal watchword: "No taxation without representation." The practice of the South African Republic is that one class has all the representation and hardly contributes to the National Revenue, while the other class, which pays the greater part of all the taxes levied, is absolutely unrepresented. Yet the advocates of the Oligarchy in Great Britain are to be found almost exclusively among those who label themselves by the time-honoured name of Liberals.

Not Party Principles, but the Welfare of South Africa Should be the Aim.

It has been necessary to show that the surrender of 1881 cannot be justified on the political theory which was professed from 1832 to 1874 by the Party which during that period led Great Britain in the transition to Democracy. The demonstration is required, because the attempt is now made by the nominal successors of that Party to represent to their followers that they are bound by their principles to the policy of 1881, the policy of surrender for the sake of what is called peace but is not. But the whole history proves, and it is one of the purposes of these chapters to assert, that the British Government, in its conduct of South African affairs, ought not to consider the theories around which our domestic controversies revolve, but ought to consider, first and above all things, the necessities and the welfare of South Africa. The settlement of 1881 was faulty because it did not and could not conduce to South Africa's good; it settled nothing; it unsettled everything.

The fundamental facts about South Africa are, that from the Cape to the Zambesi the country is geographically one, and that everywhere there is a black population far outnumbering the whites. These two conditions are permanent; they underlie everything, and they have consequences that cannot be made away with. The first consequence is that the whites must be held together. There cannot but be two castes, white and black, but the existence of two castes of whites would be a misfortune. In every country of whites and blacks the separation of the whites into two orders means the degradation of the whites excluded from the upper caste. It cannot be good for South Africa that there should be in the country two orders of whites, privileged and unprivileged; the welfare of them all, as well as of the blacks, requires that the whites should be on an equality. The welfare of the whole population requires also that the blacks should be well treated; they are, and will remain, a lower race than the whites; no legislation can lift them out of political subjection and social inferiority; but they ought to be governed for their good; their treatment by the ruling race should never lose sight of the educational aim. They have to learn to work, but they have also to be taught to be free, which means, in the first instance, to be obedient to laws.

Let us not say Peace when there is No Peace.

These are inexorable necessities of South African life. The original secessions of the Boers were a protest against the educational conception of treating the blacks, a conception that was crudely represented by early missionary zeal. The Boers with their seventeenth century notions resented the humanism of the nineteenth century. Their trek was a separation of the whites into two classes. In the Orange Free State the unity was restored. Lord Carnarvon's policy of annexation and representative government would have restored it in the Transvaal. The military governors, by withholding representative institutions and by harsh administration, renewed the breach. Mr. Gladstone, if he had reasserted British authority, and then insisted on efficient administration, could have restored it. The retrocession widened the breach between the two races. Mr. Gladstone said peace when there was no peace. To-day a new surrender is demanded by President Kruger and the Boers, by Mr. Hofmeyr and the Bond, and by the successors of Mr. Gladstone. Again the plea of peace is put forward. Mr. Gladstone patched the sore in the Transvaal, and it has festered and infected all South Africa. If the South African sore is now patched and not healed, it will grow and spread till it rends the Empire.

CHAPTER V.

THE NATURAL HISTORY OF REVOLUTION.

The Demand for Reform—Rejected it Becomes Revolution—The Raid—Effect of the Outbreak—The Moral—The New Course—Boer Misgovernment—The Aliens Expulsion Law—Outrages—The Petition to the Queen—Sir Alfred Milner's View of the Situation.

THE foundation of politics is human nature, and it is the nature of man to make a hard fight for the necessaries of life. One of the necessaries of life is a certain amount of good government; savages can do with very little, civilised men require more. The modern European expects a good deal in the way of law and administration. He has deeply rooted in him the taste for equality in the presence both of law and of its execution, and is apt to resent any manifest unfairness, especially when it touches him in pocket or person. When the system under which he lives fails to provide the minimum of these things, which he has learnt to regard as requisite and necessary as well for the body as for the soul, the modern European man is disturbed—he ventilates his grievances. A multitude with a grievance is apt to be troublesome, and most modern systems provide some kind of safety valve as an outlet for the heat generated. When there is no safety valve there is apt to be an explosion. This is the natural history of revolution, which never arises by spontaneous generation. When Europeans began to go in large numbers to the Transvaal, beginning perhaps in 1882, they probably never gave a thought to political conditions; if they did they would consult the Conventions, by which they found themselves entitled to live in the country and to carry on manufacture, trade, and commerce without liability to any taxes other than those imposed on citizens, and on a careless reading they might have thought themselves entitled to all civil rights, though in fact the Conventions of 1881 and of 1884 guarantee "all civil rights" only to persons who held property before the war of 1881, or who were loyal to the Queen during that war. The idea of permanently settling in the Transvaal might not at first have entered the minds of the newcomers, but when they had found regular work, when they were making a good living, marrying and settling down, they would naturally want to stop where they were. In 1894 there were seventy-eight thousand of these foreign residents, sixty-two thousand of whom were British subjects. In 1897 Mr. Bryce estimated them at one hundred and eighty thousand, of whom one hundred and fifty thousand spoke English. At that time, again according to Mr. Bryce, they possessed between them 63 per cent. of the landed and 90 per cent. of the personal property in the country.

The Demand for Reform.

In 1892 the British residents found that the modicum of good government supplied was below the standard to which they were accustomed. They adopted a reasonable and modest method of asking for more. A number of them founded a National Union at Johannesburg, drew up a statement of their grievances in the Dutch language, and distributed it among the Burghers. In August they held a public meeting and passed resolutions, which were laid before President Kruger by a deputation. President Kruger said to the deputation: "Cease holding public meetings and be satisfied; go back and tell your people I shall never give them anything." Further meetings were held, and in 1894 a petition signed by thirteen thousand persons, and asking for the franchise, was addressed to the President and Volksraad. The prayer of the petition was rejected. In 1895 a petition again asking for the franchise and addressed to the President and Volksraad was signed by thirty-eight thousand five hundred persons. This petition was also rejected.

Rejected it Becomes Revolution.

The President and Volksraad saw no need for a safety valve; there was therefore bound to be an explosion. Mr. Bryce, who was in the Transvaal in November, 1895, says:—

"Though I did not know that the catastrophe was so near at hand it was easy to see that a conflict must come.... The motives of these Reformers were simple and patent. Those of them who had been born or lived long in Africa thought it an intolerable wrong that, whereas everywhere else in South Africa they could acquire the suffrage and the means of influencing the Government after two or three years' residence, they were in the Transvaal condemned to a long disability, and denied all voice in applying the taxes which they paid. Thinking of South Africa as practically one country, they complained that here, and here only, were they treated as aliens and inferiors. Both they and all the other Uitlanders had substantial grievances to redress. Food was inordinately dear, because a high tariff had been imposed on imports. Water supply, police, and sanitation were all neglected. Not only was Dutch the official language, but in the public schools Dutch was the only medium of instruction; and English children were compelled to learn arithmetic, geography, and history out of Dutch text-books. It was these abuses . . . that disposed them to revolt against a Government which they despised."

A revolution, however, cannot be made with rosewater, for it implies the use of force to overthrow the obnoxious system. The Uitlanders were more numerous than the Burghers, but the Burghers were armed and the Uitlanders unarmed. The plan adopted by the leaders was to smuggle into Johannesburg two or three thousand rifles and a Maxim gun, to give out that they had arms for the whole population of the town, and in this way to bluff the Government into the concession of their demands. The manifesto which was to start the revolution, and which was published on December 26th, enumerated the grievances. It said:—

"We want: 1. The establishment of this Republic as a true Republic.

"2. A Grondwet or Constitution, which shall be framed by competent persons selected by representatives of the whole people, and framed on lines laid down by them, a Constitution which shall be safeguarded against hasty alteration.

"3. An equitable Franchise Law and fair representation.

"4. Equality of the Dutch and English languages.

"5. Responsibility to the Legislature of the heads of the great Departments.

"6. Removal of religious disabilities.

"7. Independence of the Courts of Justice, with adequate and secured remuneration of the Judges.

"8. Liberal and comprehensive education.

"9. An efficient Civil Service, with adequate provision for pay and pension.

"10. Free trade in South African products."

The method by which the revolutionaries expected to get what they wanted was an armed rising, of which they hoped that the Burghers would be so afraid that negotiation would be possible. The Burghers were afraid, or, at least, were gulled into the belief that Johannesburg was fully armed, but the revolution was shipwrecked by an intrigue which was essentially foreign to its nature.

The Raid.

The leaders had been in communication with Mr. Rhodes and through him with Dr. Jameson, and it had been arranged that Dr. Jameson's forces of the Chartered Company should, after the revolution had broken out, invade the Transvaal on the pretext of protecting the women and children. Apparently it was intended in this way to drag the British Government, to which the Chartered Company was responsible, into the imbroglio. At the last moment there was a division among the revolutionaries. The original intention was simply to secure the redress of grievances; it was now complicated by the attempt of one party to use the revolution as a pretext or occasion for undoing the retrocession of 1881. This plan, foisted on to the original movement, was a fatal complication. It involved disloyalty both to Great Britain and to the movement for the redress of grievances. It was a crime, both against the cause of the Uitlanders and against the British name. It was also a blunder, for at the last moment the leaders were paralysed by a division of opinion which, though it was settled, and rightly settled, on the understanding that the idea of annexation was to be dropped, caused delay and hesitation. Meanwhile Dr. Jameson made his first great mistake, and invaded the country prematurely. He then made his second mistake, that of being defeated, and his third, that of surrendering. The first result of the Raid was that the British Government rightly and necessarily disavowed it, ordered the leaders to withdraw, and sent the High Commissioner to ask Johannesburg to lay down its arms. Johannesburg, thoroughly bewildered, took time to consider, and then agreed to accept, as the guarantee that their grievances would be redressed, the pledge of the High Commissioner that the British Government would insist on the consideration of their grievances. The raid embarrassed not only the reformers but the British Government, for it was necessary that Great Britain, before taking up the cause of the Uitlanders, should purge herself of the suspicion of complicity in the invasion of the Transvaal.

Effect of the Outbreak.

The explosion had taken place and had not destroyed the system, but it had one good result. It attracted the attention of the world to the condition of the Transvaal, and it revealed to the people of Great Britain the fact, which ought to have been brought home to them sooner, that they have a duty towards South Africa and to their fellow-subjects who, in a State that owes its existence to British forbearance or to the weakness of a British Government, are treated as foreigners are nowhere treated within the British Empire.

The Moral.

The unfortunate events which have just been described ought, like the previous passages of South African history, to leave their lessons on our minds. Here again the reader must draw his balance-sheet, remembering that the only practical value of events past lies in the illustration which they afford of how the British Government ought to act and how it ought not to act. Can it be wrong to say that the Revolution of

1895 would have been prevented if the British Government had been attending to South Africa, and had undertaken in time to secure the redress of the grievances which caused the rising? Was it not a sin of omission for the British Government to remain a passive spectator after the rejection of the Uitlanders' petition of 1895?

The New Course.

At any rate, in 1897 the Government took a wise step in selecting Sir Alfred Milner, whom they judged to be the ablest of the younger generation of public servants, to be Governor of the Cape and High Commissioner for South Africa. Sir Alfred Milner's course has hitherto abundantly justified that estimate. No one can suggest that he has rushed into a policy or attempted to carry out a preconceived theory; for two years the British public heard nothing of him. He was unostentatiously and unsensationally studying his problem. When at the close of 1898 he paid a short visit to England, no doubt for the purpose of laying before the Government his view of the situation, and of assuring himself that he possessed their confidence, he had made himself in the best sense of the word the man on the spot.

Boer Misgovernment.

The Blue-book which was published in June 1899, contains the record of Sir Alfred Milner's observations, during something like two years, of the working of the Transvaal Government, and of its relation to the Uitlanders. It is marked throughout by an exactitude and scrupulosity of statement which prove that Sir Alfred Milner cannot be induced, even by the extraordinary nature of the facts which he has to chronicle, to commit himself to rash or exaggerated language. More remarkable still than the quiet clearness of Sir Alfred Milner's despatches is the story of misgovernment which they tell. In 1897 the Volksraad Government appointed an Industrial Commission to inquire into the situation of the mining industry and its treatment by the Government. The Commission reported that the mining industry was the financial basis, support, and mainstay of the State; it condemned the monopolies by which the industrial prosperity of the country was hampered; it condemned the tariff by which necessary articles of consumption were rendered dear; it declared that the mining industry had real grievances in connection with the administration of the liquor law, owing to the illicit sale of strong drink to the natives at the mines; it condemned the dynamite concessions; it declared that, owing to bad administration of the law, the mining industry was suffering from thefts of gold to the amount of three-quarters of a million sterling per annum. But when the Report was laid before the Volksraad, that body referred it to a Committee, which, in a long and obscure document, contemptuously set aside the recommendations. The Volksraad, instead of giving redress to the industrial population, decided to subject them to an additional tax, though the revenue of the State derived from the Uitlanders is larger than the State can spend on its administration. Great sums, of which no account is rendered, are believed to disappear into the pockets of the Boers. This is a charge which from its nature is difficult to prove, but by those who live in the Transvaal it is believed, and the Government, of which the administrative inefficiency is as notorious as its hostile spirit to the unenfranchised foreigners, is rendered the more unpopular because the foreign residents are convinced that it is also corrupt, and corrupt at their expense.

The Aliens Expulsion Law.

In 1896 the Volksraad passed an Act empowering President Kruger to expel from the Transvaal any stranger "dangerous to public peace and order," without the stranger being permitted to appeal to the Courts of Justice. The British Government pointed out that this Act violated the Convention of 1884. But in 1898 a new Act to the same effect was passed, so that Article XIV. of the Convention has been made a dead letter by the Boer Legislature.

Outrages.

A large part of the Blue-book is occupied with the details of the incredible brutality with which the Boer officials have treated coloured British subjects or "Cape Boys." Then follows the history of the shooting of Edgar and of the murder of Mrs. Applebe at Johannesburg. Edgar thought himself insulted by a drunken man, whom he knocked down. He then went into his own house and locked the door. A party of police came up and broke open the door of Edgar's house. As soon as it was broken and Edgar seen standing inside, one of the police, before a word had been spoken, shot him dead. The policeman was acquitted by the Boer Court. Some weeks later Mrs. Applebe, the wife of a Wesleyan Minister at Johannesburg, was going to church with a Mr. Wilson, when they were attacked by a gang. Each was felled by a blow and left insensible, and Mrs. Applebe died a few days afterwards of the injury received. Mr. Applebe had been a prominent advocate of reform in the administration of the liquor law, and it is believed that the murderous assault on his wife and his friend was an act of revenge for his criticisms on the illicit sellers of drink. No attempt seems to have been made to discover and punish the criminals until the remonstrances of the British agent induced the Transvaal Government to offer a reward for information. To this day the criminals are undiscovered.

The killing of Edgar and the acquittal of the policeman caused great excitement in Johannesburg, and the Uitlanders arranged to hold a public meeting, as they were lawfully entitled to do. But at the instigation of Government officials a number of workmen in Government employ were posted in the hall in order to break up the meeting. A number of Burghers and Magistrates were present, and in their presence and without remonstrance from them the meeting was violently broken up by the workmen and a number of Uitlanders assaulted. This was in January.

The Petition to the Queen.

In March the petition of the Uitlanders to the Queen was drawn up and signed by twenty-one thousand British subjects. It set forth their grievances, the futility of all their attempts to obtain redress, and asked for inquiry, for the reform of abuses, and for guarantees to be obtained from the Transvaal Government for the recognition of their rights as British subjects.

Sir Alfred Milner's View of the Situation.

In a telegram dated the 4th of May the High Commissioner expressed his view of a situation which had by that time become critical. The movement which in 1895 had taken the form of unsuccessful revolution had since that time renewed its strength. None of the grievances then complained of had been remedied, but fresh ones had been added. The action of the Volksraad in making its own resolutions binding on the Law Courts had broken the confidence of the Uitlanders in the Transvaal High Court of Judicature. The Uitlanders, while bearing the chief burden of taxation, found the law a chaos and the administration incompetent. They felt that this state of things would be remedied if they were themselves enfranchised. They felt deeply the personal indignity involved in their permanent subjection to a ruling caste which owed its wealth to their exertions. After this preamble the High Commissioner gave, in a few lines, his view of the South African situation:

"The political turmoil in the Transvaal Republic will never end till the permanent Uitlander population is admitted to a share in the Government, and while that turmoil lasts there will be no tranquillity or adequate progress in Her Majesty's South African dominions. The relations between the British Colonies and the two Republics are intimate to a degree which one must live in South Africa in order fully to realise. Socially, economically, ethnologically, they are all one country, the two principal white races are everywhere inextricably mixed up; it is absurd for either to dream of subjugating the other. The only condition on which they can live in harmony and the country progress is equality all round. South Africa can prosper under two, three, or six Governments, but not under two absolutely conflicting social and political systems, perfect equality for Dutch and British in the British Colonies side by side with permanent subjection of British to Dutch in one of the Republics. It is idle to talk of peace and unity under such a state of affairs. It is this which makes the internal condition of the Transvaal Republic a matter of vital interest to Her Majesty's Government. No merely local question affects so deeply the welfare and peace of her South African possessions. And the right of Great Britain to intervene to secure fair treatment of the Uitlanders is fully equal to her supreme interest in securing it. The majority of them are her subjects, whom she is bound to protect."

Sir Alfred Milner considered two possible courses from which a remedy might be sought. The first was that the British Government should base its action on its right to protect its own subjects. This would involve constantly-repeated remonstrances on a hundred and one different wrongs, each taken in isolation; and the refusal of redress on any one point could be met only by war. For this reason, and because such a system of perpetual nagging could hardly lead to real improvement, Sir A. Milner thought that the true remedy was to obtain a fair measure of representation for the Uitlanders. No doubt if that were obtained the Uitlanders would cease to be British subjects; but their admission to a fair share of political power would give stability to the Transvaal Republic, would remove the causes of quarrel between it and Great Britain, and would, in the long run, "entirely remove that intense suspicion and bitter hostility to Great Britain which at present dominates its external and internal policy." He went on to say that the policy of leaving things alone which has been tried for years had led to their going from bad to worse. He pointed out that the spectacle of thousands of British subjects kept permanently in the position of helots constantly chafing under undoubted grievances, and calling vainly to Her Majesty's Government for redress, does steadily undermine the influence and reputation of Great Britain and the respect for the British Government within the Queen's dominions. He referred to the fact of which his earlier despatches had given evidence, that there is in South Africa a propaganda of disloyalty among the Dutch, that the Afrikander Bond openly preaches an offensive policy, the repudiation of British supremacy, and the prevention of redress to the Uitlanders until Great Britain has surrendered her rights. In his opinion the right way to put an end to this propaganda would be for the British Government to give proof alike of its power and its justice by obtaining for the Uitlanders in the Transvaal a fair share in the government of the country which owes everything to their exertions. This course, he held, " would certainly go to the root of the political unrest in South Africa, and though temporarily it might aggravate it, it would ultimately extinguish the race feud which is the great bane of the country."

CHAPTER VI.

BLOEMFONTEIN.

The Bloemfontein Conference—President Kruger's Attitude —Why the Conference was Broken Off—President Kruger's Attitude Still Unchanged—The Actual Situation—The Parting of the Ways.

A British citizen's duty at the present time is to think out what the Government ought to do. He must put himself in Mr. Chamberlain's place, and must make up his mind what in that place he would now do. As a preliminary it is evidently fair to begin by noting exactly what Mr. Chamberlain's attitude is. In a despatch dated May 10th Mr. Chamberlain laid down the basis of the Government's policy: "Having regard to the position of Great Britain as the Paramount Power in South Africa, and the duty incumbent on them (the Government) to protect all British subjects residing in a foreign country, they cannot permanently ignore the exceptional and arbitrary treatment to which their fellow-countrymen and others are exposed, and the absolute indifference of the Government of the Republic to the friendly representations which have been made to them on the subject." The British Government, however, was most anxious that the matter should be settled amicably, it hoped that President Kruger would see his way to meet its wishes, and accordingly the despatch just quoted authorised Sir Alfred Milner to arrange for a meeting with the President. On the same day the President of the Orange Free State independently suggested that the High Commissioner and President Kruger might meet as his guests at Bloemfontein. Mr. Chamberlain authorised the High Commissioner to accept the invitation "in the hope that, in concert with the President, you may arrive at such an arrangement as Her Majesty's Government could accept and recommend to the Uitlander population as a reasonable concession to their just demands." The invitation was accordingly accepted, and in a telegram of the 22nd of May Sir Alfred Milner explained to Mr. Chamberlain the spirit in which he approached the negotiations. He thought the Uitlanders' grievance should be put into the foreground, and he should insist that they ought to obtain some substantial degree of representation by legislation to be passed this Session. Failing that he would try, as an alternative, to obtain municipal government for the whole Rand. If this also were rejected he thought it would be useless to discuss the other questions outstanding between the two Governments, such as dynamite, violations of the Zululand Boundary, the arbitrary suppression of newspapers, and the ill-treatment of "Cape Boys." Mr. Chamberlain's brief reply was a general approval of these ideas.

The Bloemfontein Conference.

Sir Alfred Milner's duty when he went to Bloemfontein was therefore to try to bring President Kruger to such an arrangement as the Government could "recommend to the Uitlander population as a reasonable concession to their just demands." This is exactly what the High Commissioner did. He explained his object with full sincerity to President Kruger, to whom he read the following memorandum:

"There are two things I have to consider: I have to consider the prejudice of the old Burghers. I know that, even if I were to convince the President himself, he might have difficulty in convincing other people; therefore I must, in proposing something, propose something which it can be made absolutely clear to the old Burghers will not swamp them. On the other hand, I have to consider that it is perfectly useless to propose something which will give no satisfaction whatever to the reasonable desires of the new population, which may be rejected at once as totally insufficient, the whole object of the proposal being to give them such an amount of satisfaction as will bring them on to the side of the State, to throw in their lot with it, and to work in future with the old Burghers as one people."

This is as clear as noonday. The High Commissioner wants to end the troubles. He wants to propose something which will satisfy the Uitlanders without injuring the Burghers or disturbing the independence of the State. He therefore proposed that any Uitlander of five years' residence who should be willing to undertake the obligations of citizenship and to defend the independence of the Republic should, on taking the oath of allegiance to the Republic, become a Burgher. He thought it reasonable that a property qualification and a good character should be required. He added that to enable the proposed enfranchisement to be of practical use a certain number of new constituencies should be formed. From his telegram to Mr. Chamberlain we know that he thought there should be not less than seven new constituencies, so as to give the Uitlanders one-fifth of the representation. The present number of members is twenty-eight; seven added makes thirty-five, of which the seven would be one-fifth. But he waited to go into detail about the new constituencies until he should find what reception the President gave to his proposals.

President Kruger's Attitude.

President Kruger had not gone there with any idea of meeting the wishes of the British Government. On the contrary, he made large demands of his own. He never so much as discussed Sir Alfred Milner's proposals, but after a day to think them over announced that any reform of the franchise was conditional on the British Government agreeing to submit disputes to arbitration and allowing him to annex Swaziland. If the High Commissioner would submit these demands to the British Government the President would submit a Bill to the Volksraad giving the franchise after seven years, two of waiting and five of naturalisation. For settlers before 1890 he would allow naturalisation within six months, followed by the franchise two years after that. Next day Sir Alfred Milner explained what he thought was unsatisfactory in the President's offer. He recognised that a seven years' term was better than one twice as long, and that a vote in two years from now was better than nothing at all. Yet he said :—

"I wish to be moderate, but I cannot recommend to other people a plan which I feel certain will not succeed. Under this plan no man who is not already naturalised, even if he has been in the country thirteen or fourteen years, will get a vote for the First Volksraad in less than two and a half years from the passing of the new law. There will be no considerable number of people obtaining that vote in less than five years, that is if they come and naturalise. But I fear that the majority of them will not come in, because the scheme retains that unfortunate provision, first introduced in 1890, by which, owing to the two stages—first, naturalisation with a partial franchise, and then, after five years, full franchise—a man has to abandon his old citizenship before he becomes a full-fledged citizen of his new country. My plan avoided this. My doctrine is that, however long a period of residence you fix before a man becomes a citizen of your State, you should admit him, once for all, to full rights on taking the oath of allegiance. And this is especially important in the South African Republic, because owing to the facility and frequency with which laws—even fundamental laws—are altered, the man who takes the oath, and thereby loses his old country, will never feel quite sure that something may not happen in the interval, when he is only half a citizen, to prevent his becoming a whole one."

The President's proposals offered no new seats to the Uitlanders, and Sir Alfred Milner was driven to the conclusion that "so far as the Uitlander Question is concerned the Conference has been productive of no result." Next day the President offered three new seats. But the High Commissioner, after consideration, did not feel that the scheme as thus amended was one of which he could advise the acceptance as a definite settlement of the difficulties that had arisen in connection with the discontent of the Uitlander population.

Why the Conference was Broken Off.

He again explained his point of view in language which cannot be too closely studied :—

"The President seemed to regard my scheme as a very alarming one. I do not think it alarming, but I admit it involved a considerable change of policy. But it is no use proposing any small change. This Conference is a very exceptional thing. The situation is grave, else we would not be discussing here. If I have urged the Government of the South African Republic to take a considerable step to allay the discontent among a large portion of the inhabitants, it is because of my firm conviction that no small measure would any longer be of any use. The Government had much to atone for in its past treatment of the Uitlanders, and it has much, indeed, it has everything, to gain in silencing their present complaints and in removing the long list of Uitlander grievances from the field of controversy between Her Majesty's Government and the South African Republic.

"The President evidently does not realise how far I was willing to go in the direction of compromise when I was prepared to drop all other questions connected with the position of British subjects in the South African Republic if only I could persuade him to adopt a liberal measure of enfranchisement. The position of British Uitlander subjects to Her Majesty has yet to be dealt with. It is evident that Her Majesty's Government think the complaints of the petitioners in many respects well founded, and that they are only waiting for the result of this Conference before addressing the Government of the South African Republic on the subject. When I came here I came in the hope that I might be able to report to Her Majesty's Government that measures were about to be adopted which would lead to such an improvement in the situation as to relieve Her Majesty's Government from pressing for the redress of particular grievances on the ground that the most serious causes of complaint would now gradually be removed from within."

This is the language of statesmanship and of moderation. Can those who have denounced

Sir Alfred Milner as a Hotspur have read either his language at Bloemfontein or the equally clear and moderate language of his despatches?

President Kruger's Attitude Still Unchanged.

The Conference was broken off, for it had failed of its object, which was to produce terms which the Uitlanders could be honestly advised by a British Government to accept. There was a good reason for fixing at five years the period of residence to be required, for that was the period fixed by the law of 1882 in force at the date, 1884, of the Convention of London. Sir Alfred Milner was therefore asking the President to go back to the law which existed at the time when the South African Republic was recognised by the British Government. The President refused. He will not have a large measure, and he will not change his policy. The Bill which has since been laid before the Volksraad and which has the approval of the Afrikander Bond, whose programme as we know is the overthrow of the British supremacy in South Africa, stipulates for seven years as the minimum term, and is so arranged as to prevent the enfranchisement at once of any but Uitlanders of more than nine years' standing.

The Actual Situation.

The facts of the situation may now be summed up. The Transvaal State owes its existence to the Convention of 1881, which was to guarantee self-government to the inhabitants of the country. At present the laws are made and administered by a Volksraad which represents one quarter of the inhabitants. The remaining three-quarters are treated as aliens. To them is due the prosperity of the country. In 1885 its revenue was £178,000; it is now £4,000,000. This revenue is almost entirely taken from the Uitlanders. The President of the Chamber of Mines is a Frenchman, M. Rouliot. He said in November, 1898: "We are the most heavily taxed community in the world, though we are the one that has the least to say about the use of the funds it contributes." During recent years more than two millions sterling has been advanced by the Transvaal Government to its officials and has not been accounted for. This Government, which has long ceased to represent the majority of the inhabitants, has violated the Conventions in virtue of which it exists, by its concession of the dynamite monopoly, by its Press Law, and by its Aliens Expulsion Law. Its administration is inefficient, being either dishonest or incompetent; for under its authority gold is stolen to the extent of three-quarters of a million a year; the law forbids the sale of drink to natives at the mines, yet 30 per cent. of the native miners are constantly drunk. Coloured British subjects are dragged from their beds at night, assaulted, and put in prison, merely because they are without a pass, and the remonstrances of the British Government on this subject are unheeded. A British subject, Edgar, was shot dead by a policeman, who, with three others, proposed to arrest him on a mere hearsay charge which proved untrue, and without so much as a word of explanation before the shooting. The policeman was acquitted in presence of a judge who commended him for doing his duty. A lawful meeting of British subjects was violently dispersed by roughs without any interference from the police. The Courts of Justice have been deprived of their independence and made subordinate to the Executive.

In these conditions the British subjects feel that they have not the security for person and property to which their British birthright entitles them. No constitutional method of redress is open to them within the Transvaal. They are under disabilities that have been created since the Convention of 1884 by special enactments for the purpose of excluding them from any share in the self-government guaranteed by the Conventions to the State. Mr. Chamberlain has declared, as a Minister of the Crown, that the British subjects and the Uitlanders generally have substantial grounds for their complaints, which he has summed up by saying that under present conditions, all of which have arisen since the Convention of 1884 was signed, they are now denied that equality of treatment which the Convention was designed to secure for them.

Sir Alfred Milner has shown how the unrest thus created in the Transvaal necessarily causes unrest throughout South Africa.

The British Government has attempted to

obtain a settlement by urging on President Kruger a broad measure by which the disabilities under which the Uitlanders labour may be at once removed, so that by the establishment of harmony within the State the reasons which would otherwise compel Great Britain to interfere might disappear. President Kruger has not responded to that appeal.

The Parting of the Ways.

There were two courses foreshadowed in Mr. Chamberlain's despatch instructing the High Commissioner to arrange a meeting with the President, and set forth in Sir Alfred Milner's memorandum read to President Kruger at the close of the Bloemfontein Conference. The normal course was to address the Transvaal Government with regard to its treatment of British subjects, and its repeated violation of the Conventions, on which its existence is based. It is evident that remonstrances of this kind, if unheeded, must be followed by action, and in this case the action could only be the occupation of the country. But the British Government thought that before this course was adopted the attempt should be made to induce President Kruger to remedy of his own accord the grievances of the Uitlanders. This attempt has failed. The British Government, therefore, must either let the matter drop, or adopt the normal course by demanding that British subjects shall be treated according to British law, and in case that is not done, by occupying the country, and thus taking an effective guarantee for their protection. These are the only two courses, and a choice has to be made between them. Either course must have serious consequences, and yet a decision must be taken. If Great Britain sits still and does nothing, she renounces before all the world the duty of protecting her own citizens, and with it the directing influence which she has hitherto believed herself to hold in South Africa. If, on the other hand, she keeps to her purpose of fulfilling her duty to her subjects, and of carrying out her Imperial task in South Africa, it is open to President Kruger to force on her a war which may be costly and troublesome, and may involve greater sacrifices than are at first sight apparent. The nation has reached a point where two roads diverge, and one of the two must be followed. The people of Great Britain have to make the choice, and to answer for it to their children, to their kinsmen of the Colonies, and to their own conscience and good sense.

CHAPTER VII.

The Straightforward Policy.

Effect of Arousing the Sentiment of Nationality—The Wisdom of the Bloemfontein Programme — The Courses: To the Left—To the Right—And Straight Forward—Difficulties of a Firm Policy—Its Advantages—British Democracy on its Trial.

The history of South Africa illustrates the action and reaction between practical grievances and national sentiment. The Dutch or Boer sentiment at the Cape derived its nourishment from the attempt, too often repeated, to govern a distant Colony in accordance with the abstract and one-sided doctrines developed in Downing Street or at Exeter Hall. Efficient government covers a multitude of sins, but efficient government means the application of good sense and a strong will to actual conditions, and for fifty years the ordinary practice of Cabinets has been to govern Colonies according to the catchwords which would bring votes at home; only on rare occasions have they risen to the consideration of the needs of a Colony. Let us do justice to the Boers and admit that the Great Trek was brought about by the neglect of British Governments to direct their policy in accordance with South African conditions. The Trek was a protest against unsympathetic administration, and it involved the development of a national sentiment, or at any rate, of a Boer prejudice against the British. The Transvaal rising of 1881 cannot be attributed to Boer national feeling or Boer prejudice alone, but to the stimulus given to that feeling or that prejudice by vacillating, inefficient, and, to use once more a mild term, unsympathetic administration.

Effect of Arousing the Sentiment of Nationality.

The grant of self-government to the Transvaal after the Boer successes could not but be a great encouragement to the Boer feeling of nationality. It is perfectly natural that since then the Boers should have tenaciously clung to their independence, that they should be profoundly mistrustful of the Uitlanders, and that they should regard their liberty as bound up with the maintenance of their own monopoly of political rights. But the Transvaal is not the whole of South Africa, and it is impossible for it to be socially and politically isolated from the neighbouring countries. Mr. Gladstone, by stipulating that the self-government which he granted should be accompanied by a British suzerainty, may have thought that he was preserving the unity of South Africa, but what he hoped to secure by suzerainty he undermined by the recognition of self-government, for he thereby set up in the mind of every Dutchman at the Cape the ideal of Afrikander independence. Suzerainty and independence are incompatible terms. Mr. Gladstone left them to fight out their own battles, and the result is the situation of to-day.

Nationality, it may be observed, cuts two ways, for there is a British as well as a Boer national sentiment. If there is to be a Boer nation in the Transvaal it is impossible to suppress the aspiration for a Boer nation in the Cape Colony, and impossible also to prevent the accentuation of British national sentiment in Natal and Rhodesia. An exclusively Boer nation in the Transvaal means the permanent division of South Africa into two hostile camps, a division that cannot possibly conduce to the welfare of the country. And if the feeling of Boer nationality was stimulated by inefficient British administration, the inefficiency of Boer administration has stirred up in turn the national feeling of the British.

The Wisdom of the Bloemfontein Programme.

It is the mark of Sir Alfred Milner's statesmanship, of his complete grasp of the whole problem with which he has to deal, that at Bloemfontein he proposed an arrangement by which the principle of nationality would have its edge blunted; he saw that the moment a reasonable proportion of the Uitlanders are transformed into Burghers and are given a visible share, even a small share, in the government of the Transvaal, they will become as stout defenders of the Republican institutions of that State as are the Burghers of Boer descent. The question will no longer be Boer or British, but will be the effective administration of the Transvaal, and when the question, Boer or British, has been buried in the Transvaal, it will die a natural death in the rest of South Africa. This is the real meaning of the proposals made on the part of Great Britain at Bloemfontein, of which the object was to unite and not to divide South Africans. If President Kruger sincerely wishes for peace and for a settlement, he will end by accepting as the preliminary the Bloemfontein demand for a five years' retrospective enfranchising law, together with the formation of seven new seats for the Uitlanders, and with additional new Uitlander seats in the proportion of one to five for all new Boer seats that he may wish to create. It is only by steadfastly maintaining the demand which has been made that a peaceful settlement is to be obtained; any other course may be peaceful in the sense of avoiding bloodshed for the present, but will involve a continuance of the prevailing unrest, with all its possibilities of conflict.

THE COURSES: TO THE LEFT—

Jomini used to say that a commander in war had usually to settle a very simple question:

whether to go to the right, to the left, or straight forward. The same maxim may be applied to the statesman in matters of policy. In the case before us there is a school that would go to the left, and would leave the Uitlanders in the lurch for no other reason than that insistence on justice may possibly involve the use of arms. This school, in so far as it is the honest outcome of an excess of humanitarianism, may perhaps be neglected, for its adherents if consistent must think it right to stand by and see their women insulted rather than knock down the ruffians who would molest them. When humanitarianism defies commonsense it is beyond the reach of argument. But there is another section that disguises disloyalty in the humanitarian garb. There has been too much talk of peace by persons connected with the Afrikander Bond, whose object is not peace, but the destruction of British influence in South Africa.

TO THE RIGHT—

The opposite extreme is that of the school which would force on a war in order to undo the concession of 1881 and to recover the Transvaal as a British Colony. This is not the policy of Sir Alfred Milner. It is utterly inconsistent with the scheme of enfranchisement which he propounded at Bloemfontein. It is not the policy of the Government nor of the majority of the people of the United Kingdom. But if President Kruger does not shortly accept the compromise offered him at the Conference he may drive the British Government into action which would have the same result as this policy.

AND STRAIGHT FORWARD.

The only honourable course, after the Government's declarations prior to the Conference and after what there took place, is to insist on the acceptance by the South African Republic of the Bloemfontein proposals, and to back up that insistence by adequate military preparations. This is the policy which the Government appears to be pursuing, and which must commend itself to all who are neither Afrikanders nor believers in peace at any price. If it is to be effective the preparations should go steadily on as though war had been declared by the Transvaal; there should be no interruption in the movement of troops or in any of the arrangements until a settlement has been effected and the Government is satisfied that it will be honestly and fairly carried out.

But suppose President Kruger will not agree to the British terms? In that case there is no choice but to pass from the preparation of arms to their use. For a persistent refusal to relieve the Uitlanders of their disabilities will render necessary British intervention. There is no need to enter into subtle arguments about the word Suzerainty. Both the Convention of 1881 and 1884 contain stipulations whereby Great Britain asserts her right both to supervise the foreign policy of the Transvaal, and to secure fair treatment for the coloured natives as well as for the European settlers other than Burghers. All these stipulations imply that Great Britain is the Paramount Power. If now she fails to assert that position her omission will be considered as its renunciation; the Afrikander Bond will agitate for the independence of South Africa, and the British subjects throughout the country, feeling deserted by their own Government, will make common cause with the members of the Bond. The loss of South Africa to the Empire can then be a question only of a comparatively short time.

Difficulties of a Firm Policy.

It is clear that if President Kruger allows matters to come to the point of war the whole conditions will be changed. If once a shot is fired there can be no truce or peace without the defeat of the Boer forces, and after that there would be no question of the restoration of the South African Republic. But that is for President Kruger to consider, and for his friends of the Bond who have promised him their "moral support" after his refusal of Sir Alfred Milner's proposals. No doubt a war against the Transvaal would have its difficulties and its serious consequences for Great Britain. The Boers would count on the sympathy—perhaps even on the help—of the Orange Free State and of the Afrikander Bond in the Cape Colony. While the Boers would be fighting for their political existence, Great Britain on her part could not afford to fail, so that a contest once begun would have to be fought out. The Boers as sharpshooters and skirmishers excel in two essentials of modern warfare, but they can hardly have the discipline and organisation of an army. The British Government would have to employ a thoroughly efficient force, not less than an army corps, and to spend money freely upon transport, in order to secure prompt and uninterrupted victory. Success in the field would be followed by prolonged difficulties. It would at first be accompanied by great embitterment between the two races, and the necessity of reorganising the Transvaal as a British Colony—for, as has been said, after a war the Transvaal could not be left independent—would make it necessary to keep a strong garrison in the country for several years.

Its Advantages.

These are the dark shades of the picture. But there is also a bright side. So soon as it is seen that Great Britain will and can assert her authority in South Africa, the disloyalty now seething in the Cape Colony will hide its head. So soon as victory had been followed by equal justice, and it was seen that the British purpose is not to oppress the Boers, but to give fair and equal treatment both to Boer and Uitlander, the bitterness would begin to pass away and there would be peace. Of course, there can be neither success nor settlement if Great Britain, having once begun to assert her authority, should hesitate or vacillate. It will be necessary to support Sir Alfred Milner, as Lord Cromer has been supported in Egypt, until his task is accomplished and he can report that Dutch and British are satisfied and have put away their rivalry.

The situation calls for a prompt settlement, not in the way of compromise, which has already done too much harm in South Africa, but by the removal of the cause of disturbance, the inequality of status between the British and the Boers in the Transvaal. If the Transvaal Government will comply with the needs of the case, the crisis will thereby come to an end. Failing that, Great Britain must enforce the principle of equality.

British Democracy on its Trial.

There is no question of party involved in the matter, and it would be deplorable if party issues were raised. It is a great national and

Imperial issue, involving the welfare of South Africa, the spirit of unity throughout the Empire, and the character of the Nation. For, as was said in the first chapter, the task of the democratic form of government in these days, at any rate in Great Britain, is to prove its ability to conduct the affairs of an Empire. Thucydides puts into the mouth of Cleon the opinion that a democracy cannot possibly govern dependencies, and gives as the reasons partly that a democratic public is prone to suppose that its adversaries are always acting in good faith, when in fact they are often concealing hostile intentions under fair words, and partly that a democracy will not understand that if you are to govern you must be the master, and sometimes strike hard. In a later age Machiavelli attributed the success of the Romans in building up their Empire to their never having shirked a war nor postponed a conflict which they saw to be inevitable. The British aristocracy of the Eighteenth Century had something of the Roman strength; the British democracy of to-day is not without the Athenian weakness. Yet Great Britain's task resembles that of Rome; she has to give to the lands which acknowledge her influence her system of government of which the name is freedom. If she is to do this she must assert her influence against challenge—such as that of the Afrikander Bond, which is now using the Boers as an instrument—and must maintain it by exerting it for the benefit of those over whom it is spread.

It may be and perhaps is impossible for the mass of voters, to whom in a democracy the ultimate appeal lies, to acquire in regard to each Colony and every foreign country the full knowledge on which alone good government can be based. But unless the voters are determined to entrust authority only to those who have the necessary knowledge, Democracy must fail in the performance of its Imperial task. The problem of South Africa is a sample of the work of Empire. The Government has been guided by a sound judgment in giving authority there to a man chosen for his character and power of grasping a situation. It is for the electorate to see that the man thus chosen is upheld. Support to Sir Alfred Milner is the right solution of the difficulties in South Africa to-day, and is the clue to the way in which a democracy can manage an Empire. If we compel governments to select men according to their capacity for all the posts of authority in the administration of the Empire, we may yet refute the saying of the Athenian demagogue. But a Nation is more than its Constitution. If the democratic system fails, another will take its place. The Nation's work, the administration and defence of the Empire, must be carried on.

THE NATION'S AWAKENING.

Essays Towards a British Policy.

BY
SPENSER WILKINSON.

Crown 8vo., 3s. 6d.

CONTENTS.

Introduction: OUR PAST APATHY.

BOOK I.—THE AIMS OF THE GREAT POWERS.

i.—The Policy of France.
ii.—The Old Germany.
iii.—The New Germany.
iv.—German Policy towards France.
v.—German Policy towards Russia; the Triple Alliance.
vi.—The Effects of the Triple Alliance.
vii.—The Drift of Russian Policy.
viii.—The Present Situation.

BOOK II.—THE DEFENCE OF BRITISH INTERESTS.

i.—The Need for a Policy.
ii.—A Policy Proposed.
iii.—The Objections to an Alliance with Russia or with France and to a Policy of Isolation.
iv.—Justification of the Policy proposed.

BOOK III.—THE ORGANISATION OF GOVERNMENT FOR THE DEFENCE OF BRITISH INTERESTS.

i.—Diplomacy.
ii.—Initiative, Continuity, Comprehensiveness.
iii.—The Foreign Office.
iv.—The Prime Minister.
v.—The Problem of Imperial Defence.
vi.—The Cabinet and the Army and Navy.
vii.—The Spirit of Modern Organisation.

BOOK IV.—THE IDEA OF THE NATION.

i.—The Foundations of British Power.
ii.—The Meaning of Empire.
iii.—The Education of the British Race.

"We welcome the volume, as we have welcomed previous volumes from Mr. Wilkinson's pen, as of the highest value towards the formation of a national policy, of which we never stood in greater need."
—*Athenæum.*

A. CONSTABLE AND CO.
1896.

The Great Alternative:

A PLEA FOR A NATIONAL POLICY.

BY

SPENSER WILKINSON.

Small Demy 8vo., 7s. 6d.

CONTENTS.

INTRODUCTION:—I. NATIONAL PARALYSIS. II. THE REMEDY.

I. THE EASTERN QUESTION.
II. THE UNION OF GERMANY.
III. THE PARTITION OF TURKEY AND THE TRIPLE ALLIANCE.
IV. THE USE OF ARMIES.
V. THE SECRET OF THE SEA.
VI. EGYPT.
VII. A WARNING FROM GERMANY.
VIII. THE EXPANSION OF FRANCE.
IX. INDIA.
X. THE GREAT ALTERNATIVE.
XI. THE REVIVAL OF DUTY.

SATURDAY REVIEW.—" The two chapters of chief interest are those wherein the writer develops the thesis which gives its title to his book by laying *The Great Alternative* before his readers and pleading for that 'Revival of Duty' which alone can enable them to choose aright. The lucidity with which the present European situation is reviewed in these pages, and the power and acumen with which all its issues are examined, deserve unqualified praise."

SPECTATOR.—" Mr. Spenser Wilkinson's book is quite full of excellent things. Historically it is, as a rule, exceedingly strong, and one or two of the chapters can only be described as masterly. Particularly good is the résumé of Egyptian affairs. 'The Secret of the Sea' is again a perfect masterpiece of suggestive writing.... The striking thing about the details of the book is their fulness and accuracy, and the perception everywhere displayed of the realities which underlie the seeming facts of a situation. We gladly acknowledge the work to be a real contribution to political science."

LITERARY WORLD.—"One need not accept either Mr. Wilkinson's view of our statesmen, or his general conclusions, to feel that his book is a valuable one.... What the country appears to us to need is a serious and deliberate realisation of the extent and nature of our Imperial interests and responsibilities. Those interests and responsibilities must be faced as a whole, if at all, and a book like *The Great Alternative* is helpful as bringing home to the reader what politics on a large scale really mean."

SWAN SONNENSCHEIN & CO.
1894.

www.ingramcontent.com/pod-product-compliance
Lightning Source LLC
Chambersburg PA
CBHW020124170426
43199CB00009B/621